DAN MARINO

THE MAKING OF A LEGEND

Presented by Beckett Publications

DALLAS, TEXAS

Dan Marino — The Making of a Legend
Copyright ©1999 by Dr. James Beckett
All rights reserved under International and Pan-American Copyright Conventions.

Published by
Beckett Publications
15850 Dallas Parkway
Dallas, TX 75248

ISBN: 1-887432-78-7
Beckett is a registered trademark of Beckett Publications.

First Edition: August 1999
Beckett Corporate Sales and Information (972) 991-6657

CONTENTS

FOREWORD

BY TROY AIKMAN
AS TOLD TO MICKEY SPAGNOLA

The first time I was really aware of Danny was when he was a senior at Pittsburgh, so I was still in high school. He has always been, from the first time I saw him throw and saw him play, the one guy I enjoyed watching ... the one guy I would sit in front of a TV and watch play. And I've done the same at the Quarterback Challenges, too, just watching him compete.

Danny is the only active player in the NFL who I've asked for an autograph for my own collection. There has always just been something about him that I liked. As much as everyone makes such a big deal about his talents, and we all know about his delivery, the quick release, what I like most is the way he competes on the field. I like his fiery competitiveness. I think that is what drew me to really enjoy watching him play. He's just a guy I've always admired and respected as a player.

In my opinion he's the best. Sure, he's not a real mobile guy, not someone who is going to elude a lot of tackles, but the example I always use when I talk to kids is that he has great feet, some of the best feet in the game as far as getting himself in a position to deliver a football. And then I think he has the intangibles that make a great quarterback.

It's funny, because over the years I've gone from watching him

play when I was in high school, to watching him play when I was at Oklahoma, when we were in Miami for the Orange Bowl in 1984 — that was quite a thrill. Not only playing against him in the pros, but becoming part of the Quarterback Club with him, sharing some of the same endorsements and just getting to know him as a person.

I can remember the first time I competed against him, my rookie year, 1989, at Texas Stadium. That was exciting and a little different because it was the first time I can remember being on the field with somebody who I had really had looked up to, and then here I was playing against him. So it was different. And you'd better believe I watched him, too. We were on the field, and I watched him play, and he played well against us that day (passing for 255 yards and one touchdown in the Dolphins' 17–14 victory). And although I've never really put much stock in beating another quarterback, and everybody wants to do that with quarterbacks — pit them against each other even though they don't actually play against each other — I must admit, deep down, I'd say it meant something special to me when we finally beat him and the Dolphins in 1996, 29–10.

When it comes to records in general, they are pretty insignificant to me. They just aren't important to me. But Danny has played at such a high level for such a long time, I think his records are meaningful. To me, that defines greatness. And he'll continue to play as long as he can. I know some guys get burned out on the game. Some guys lose it a little bit early and can't play at the level they want to play at and get out. But I can remember the first time I talked to Danny, he said they were going to have to carry him off the field. He loves playing the game. And he's been true to that over the 10 years I've known him. And I believe that. He's one of those guys who can't see saying "I'm going to retire." It's almost like they are going to have to kick him out of the game to make him retire.

But I know deep down, before he retires, he'd like to win a Super Bowl. He makes jokes about it, but I think it affects him that he hasn't won one, and maybe affects him even more now that John Elway has won a couple. Danny and John came in together in 1983, and they are close friends and very competitive. And I think the way John was able to go out, and the Broncos certainly surrounded him with a heckuva supporting cast over the last four years of his career, Danny is hopping to hang on long enough to get that same type of supporting cast.

But you know what? If Danny never goes to another Super Bowl, or doesn't win one, no question he's still a Hall of Fame player with a tremendous career — a career that all quarterbacks would dream of having. And he would say his career is complete. Now John said the same thing, but when he won, then admitted it would not have been complete. I always would think there is something missing, but if he doesn't win a Super Bowl, that just does not take away from the player he is.

Do I pull for him to win a Super Bowl? Once we're out of the picture, yeah, I pull for him. Because when I look back on his career, as much as he's accomplished, with what he's done for the game and what he's meant to this league, I think he deserves one.

YOUTH MOVEMENT

BY PAT LIVINGSTON

idway through the 1976 season, during which his University of Pittsburgh football team won a national championship, Coach Johnny Majors was at a luncheon with his attorney in a downtown restaurant. During the course of that luncheon, Majors heard the tale of a fabulous scholastic star in his own backyard, only a stone's throw from the Pitt campus.

"This kid is unreal," said the attorney. "He's a high school sophomore; big at 6-foot-3 and 200 pounds. He's smart, got a rifle of an arm and an incredible release. He's going to be a gem for some lucky coach in a couple of years."

That prospect turned out to be Dan Marino, who at that time was playing for Central Catholic High School, only a short hike out Fifth Avenue from Majors' office in the stadium. Majors never capitalized on the youngster, however, for the following season he was coaching at Tennessee. But his successor at Pitt, Jackie Sherrill, launched a two-year vigil.

"I was really surprised that we got him," Sherrill says. "Right until the day he signed with us, I thought Dan was going into baseball. He was a heckuva ball player, drafted very high by the Kansas City Royals."

MARINO'S FATHER, DAN SR.,
DROVE A DELIVERY TRUCK FOR A
PITTSBURGH NEWSPAPER, LEAV-
ING HIS AFTERNOONS FREE FOR
TIME WITH HIS SON. DAN AND
HIS FATHER PLAYED COUNTLESS
GAMES OF CATCH IN THE BACK-
YARD. MARINO CONTINUED HIS
INTEREST IN SPORTS IN THE
FOURTH-GRADE AS A WATER BOY
FOR HIS PARISH GRADE SCHOOL,
ST. REGIS.

Sherrill didn't recall whether Johnny Majors had passed the lawyer's recommendation onto him or not.

"It didn't make any difference," Sherrill says. "A year later, every coach in the country was on to him. And most of us surmised he would opt for baseball considering the size of the contracts they were tossing around."

If he didn't sign with the Royals, the consensus was that he would enroll, naturally, at Penn State where Joe Paterno was running a college football powerhouse, or at Notre Dame where top-drawer Catholic quarterbacks frequently wound up.

But in mid-spring, at a packed press conference at his high school, Marino announced his decision. He would become a Pitt Panther. A year later, Marino became the starter midway through the season and led the Panthers to an 11–1 record and a Fiesta Bowl bid. "I felt he was going to become a great quarterback, but I didn't expect him to do it as quickly as he did," said Sherrill.

Thus Dan decided to join the long list of quarterbacks who have found their way into professional football from the Western Pennsylvania Inter-Scholastic Athletic Conference: Johnny Lujack, George Blanda, Babe Parilli, Joe Namath, Jim Kelly, Joe Montana and Terry Hanratty. Never mind those who also made it big in Canada.

One who did expect big things of Marino was Sal Sunseri, a linebacker who played with Marino at Central Catholic and later at Pitt.

"He was so focused on football that you knew he was a great one right from the start," says Sunseri, now coaching college football in Alabama. "He was always working out. Nobody worked harder than Danny did. He even talked teammates into running the hills of Schenly Park with him."

At that time, Central Catholic was a good team, but hardly a great team on the level of Butler or Penn Hills, the two major high schools that were dominating Western Pennsylvania football in the late 1970s. But those schools were well aware of Central, particularly in Marino's senior year, when Central's 9-1 record earned them a rare spot in the playoffs.

"I've been watching Marino all season, and I don't think there's a better quarterback in the country," said Andy Urbanik, the Penn Hills coach a day before the two teams met in their playoff for the league

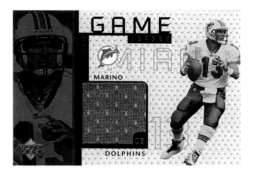

IN 1998 UPPER DECK PRODUCED THE GAME JERSEY CARD WHICH INCORPORATED A SWATCH OF AUTHENTIC GAME-WORN HOME JERSEY IN EVERY CARD.

MARINO WAS NAMED A *PARADE* ALL-AMERICAN HIS SENIOR YEAR AT CENTRAL CATHOLIC HIGH SCHOOL IN PITTSBURGH.

championship. Leading 7–0 with two minutes to play, Penn Hills clinched the victory with a last minute touchdown and stellar play of two youngsters who would later share the fruits of victory with Marino at Pitt.

They were quarterback Tom Flynn, who intercepted a key pass and later gained 34 yards of the game-ending 46-yard scoring drive and offensive tackle Bill Fralic, who threw a flattening block on one touchdown. Fralic later achieved NFL stardom with the Atlanta Falcons.

A youngster unaccustomed to losing, Marino was disconsolate after the defeat, blaming himself for the loss. Asked by a reporter if he had played a bad game, Marino replied, "Definitely."

"I don't feel he had a bad game," countered Urbanik, the winning coach. "We played an exceptional game containing him. Our inside people contained him inside the pocket. Our defense played great football."

Was that Penn Hills' best performance of the season? "It had to be." said Urbanik consolingly. "It's the best offense we saw all season."

In the packed stands, Pitt coach Jackie Sherrill was delighted

EVEN AS A JUNIOR IN HIGH SCHOOL DAN STOOD OUT FROM THE CROWD, AS YOU CAN SEE IN THIS TEAM PHOTO.

with what he had seen of both teams, but he still wasn't sure of Marino. People more familiar with such things were informing him that Marino preferred baseball to football and was likely to sign quickly if he were selected by a major league team in the spring draft.

If there was one strap left for Sherrill to hang onto, it was Marino's relationship with his family. Like most of Oakland's families in those days, the Marino clan was a closely knit group, one that fit snugly into Oakland's ethnic landscape, and it was Jackie's hope that someone in it could impress upon Danny to spend a few more years in the neighborhood. In attending Pitt, nothing would change for him.

He still would walk the same streets every day, past the Strand Theatre and the Police Station. In a few minutes he would be striding by Forbes Field, two or three blocks down the road from Pitt Stadium, and in a couple of blocks more, he would pass by the shuttered Gardens where the city's hockey teams and Duquesne's basketball teams had played. On other days, he would run into legendary Pie Traynor, who would be taking his daily walk down Fifth Avenue to his

East Brady

Beaver Falls

P E N N S Y L V A N I A

Pittsburgh

Johnstown

Youngwood

Monongahela

LOCAL HERO AND ALTAR BOY, MARINO LEFT A STRONG IMPRESSION ON HIS FORMER HIGH SCHOOL AND THE COMMUNITY. IN 1990 HIS NEIGHBORHOOD PLAYGROUND WAS OFFICIALLY RENAMED DAN MARINO FIELD.

downtown radio station. Or Dan might stop in at Frank Gustine's for a barbecue, Coke and a chat, perhaps, with a Pirate player or two.

Oakland, where Dan Marino grew up, was made up of fine, hard-working people: immigrants and first generation Yanks who made the steel and paved the roads and laid the rails that expanded Pittsburgh to its Eastern suburbs a half century before the city looked in other directions for growth. It housed the Syria Mosque where operas were presented, and the Playhouse where drama was staged, and the Soldiers and Sailors Hall that honored its citizens who fought in every war America ever fought. This is Oakland, the section of Pittsburgh where Danny Marino grew up.

And it is what Jackie Sherrill was relying on in the months he waited for Danny Marino to decide where to go and what to do after high school. In the end the University of Pittsburgh won the Dan Marino lottery.

AFTER THE SENIOR PROM AT CENTRAL CATHOLIC HIGH SCHOOL, DAN RACKED THEM UP FOR A FRIENDLY GAME OF POOL.

MARINO THE BEAR? ISSUED IN JANUARY 1999, THE DAN MARINO SALVINO'S BAMMER IS ONE OF 12 IN THE SET. HIS NAME AND JERSEY NUMBER ALSO APPEAR ON THE BACK OF THE BEAR.

[19]

A TWO-SPORT STANDOUT IN HIGH SCHOOL, MARINO WAS A FOURTH-ROUND PICK OF THE KANSAS CITY ROYALS IN THE JUNE 1979 FREE AGENT BASEBALL DRAFT. MARINO DIDN'T SIGN TO PITCH FOR THE ROYALS AND DECIDED TO STAY ON THE GRID-IRON. "THE TEMPTATION TO PLAY BASEBALL WAS TREMENDOUS," SAID MARINO. "BUT I NOT ONLY WANTED TO PLAY FOOTBALL, I WANTED AN EDUCATION."

BY SIGNING WITH THE UNIVERSITY OF PITTSBURGH, MARINO WAS ABLE TO CONTINUE HIS FOOTBALL CAREER WITHOUT HAVING TO LEAVE THE HOME IN WHICH HIS FATHER, DAN SR., AND MOTHER, VERONICA, RAISED HIM. "ALL THOSE TIMES I PLAYED FOOTBALL IN THE STREETS," SAID MARINO. "SOMETHING, MAYBE MY HEART TOLD ME TO STAY HOME AND GO TO PITT."

COLLEGE TRY

BY PAT LIVINGSTON

Having landed Danny Marino for his University of Pittsburgh football team, Jackie Sherrill had hoped that he would be able to work him slowly into the lineup. He used him sparingly in Pitt's early-season games, a series or two at a time, for Marino's predecessor, Rick Trocano, had been performing admirably. But in the sixth game, tragedy struck. Trocano was hurt and out for the season.

Rushed into the game, Marino promptly unleashed his first pass right into the arms of a Navy defender.

"But the next pass he threw, he threw it for a touchdown," said Sherrill.

That touchdown scene was to be repeated many times during the next four years as Sherrill's Panthers rolled to 30 victories in their next 33 games, including impressive triumphs in the Fiesta Bowl, the Gator Bowl, and the Sugar Bowl. Marino's last minute, fourth-down scoring pass in the 1981 Sugar Bowl convinced Georgia's skeptical fans that the Tony Dorsett-engineered Pittsburgh victory over the Bulldogs six years earlier wasn't the fluke they figured it to be.

Tim Lewis, who coaches defensive backs for the Pittsburgh

> ONE OF ONLY FOUR PLAYERS TO HAVE THEIR JERSEY RETIRED AT THE UNIVERSITY OF PITTSBURGH, MARINO THREW FOR 8,597 YARDS AND 79 TDs OVER HIS FOUR-YEAR CAREER.

EVEN EARLY IN HIS CAREER, MARINO WAS ALWAYS EAGER TO WORK WITH CHARITIES. WHETHER IT WAS THE SPECIAL OLYMPICS OR THE BOY SCOUTS, HE WAS WILLING TO LEND A HAND. THAT DEVOTION TO CHARITABLE CAUSES HAS CONTINUED WITH MARINO IN HIS PROFESSIONAL CAREER.

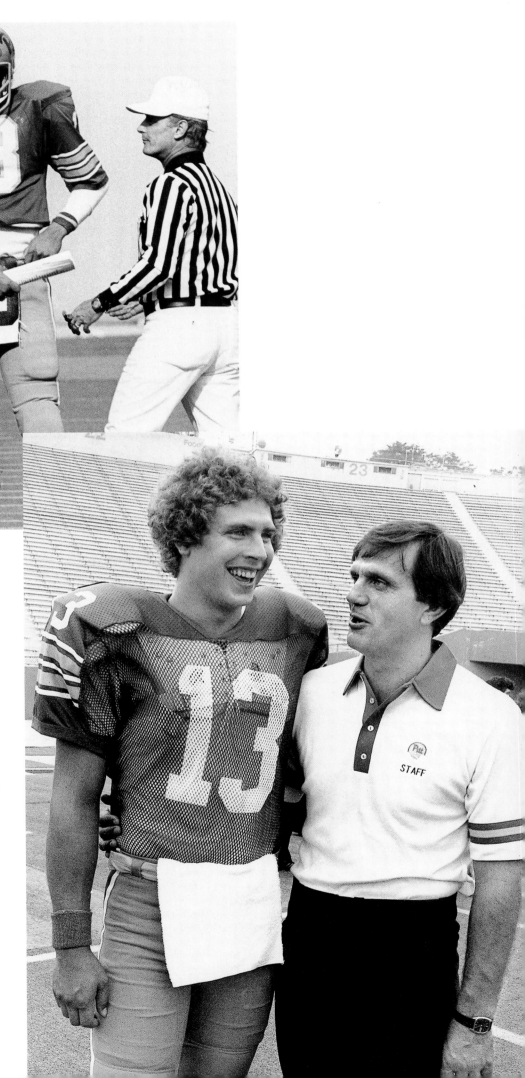

JACKIE SHERRILL WAS DELIGHTED WHEN MARINO CHOSE FOOTBALL OVER BASEBALL AND COULD HARDLY CONTAIN HIMSELF WHEN HE DECIDED TO ATTEND THE UNIVERSITY OF PITTSBURGH. AFTER WINNING THE RECRUITING BATTLE FOR MARINO, SHERRILL BECAME HIS COACH AND MENTOR UNTIL FOGE FAZIO TOOK OVER AS HEAD COACH AT PITT FOR MARINO'S SENIOR SEASON.

Steelers, is one of Marino's long term boosters, both as a football player and as a friend. They met when both played in the Big 33 Game, a post-season high school game which pits the best prospects in Western Pennsylvania against the best of the East, which includes Philadelphia and the regions where hard coal, anthracite coal, was once mined.

"I intercepted one of Danny's passes in that game; as a matter of fact, I intercepted one against him at Green Bay, too," remembered Lewis, who would wind up as one of Marino's teammates at Pitt. "I treasure the memories of those interceptions; I treasure them even more now that I know what an achievement it was to have intercepted him."

Was Danny really that good of a football player?

"As good as they get," said Lewis. "Still, I was drafted before him

"AS A PASSER, A STRATEGIST AND A LEADER, HE IS IN A CLASS BY HIMSELF," SAID JOE MOORE, THE OFFENSIVE LINE COACH AT PITT DURING MARINO'S TENURE. "THEY (THE LINEMEN) USUALLY GAVE HIM TIME TO FIND HIS RECEIVERS, BUT IF THE PROTECTION BROKE DOWN HE GOT RID OF THE BALL QUICKLY, SO IT WAS ALL BUT IMPOSSIBLE TO SACK HIM."

IN THE 1982 SUGAR BOWL, MARINO PLAYED WHAT HE CONSIDERS HIS GREATEST COLLEGE GAME. PITT TRAILED GEORGIA, 20-17, AND WAS DOWN TO A SINGLE PLAY, FOURTH AND 5 AT THE GEORGIA 33-YARD LINE. WITH TIME RUNNING OUT HE THREW IT DEEP TO HIS TIGHT END, JOHN BROWN (89), FOR THE GAME-WINNING TOUCHDOWN. AFTER THE GAME MARINO WAS NAMED MVP.

THE 1998 STARTING LINEUP CLASSIC DOUBLES — UNIVERSITY OF PITTSBURGH — IS THE ONLY STARTING LINEUP PIECE WITH HIM IN HIS PITT UNIFORM. THESE FIGURES WERE ONLY AVAILABLE AT WAL-MART AND WERE PAIRED WITH A MARINO FIGURE IN A DOLPHINS' UNIFORM.

in 1983. He wasn't drafted until the 27th pick; I was drafted 11th, and I won't let him forget that."

There must have been a number of excellent players at Pitt in those years, particularly since 30 Panthers were drafted by the NFL (11 in the first round). "Oh yeah, we had lots of good players, but we all rode Danny's coattails," conceded Lewis. "Danny was the guy who pulled the trigger.

"If he didn't get the ball off as quickly as he did, the ball wouldn't be there for his receivers. The linemen would have to hold their blocks longer and maybe they couldn't do that. Danny did so many things that made it easy to block for him. He was a ballplayer's ballplayer. Not only a great teammate, but he's been a special person to me over the years, a real friend."

If there ever was a disappointment in Marino's career at Pitt, it came on a November afternoon in 1982, as the Panthers faced their bitter rivals, Penn State. With another national championship at stake, Marino opened the game by firing touchdown passes on his first two possessions. But then on the third foray deep into Penn State territory, a Lion defender intercepted Marino's pass. After that, all hell broke loose.

MARINO LED PITT TO THREE
CONSECUTIVE 11–1 SEASONS AND
POSTSEASON APPEARANCES IN
THE FIESTA, GATOR, SUGAR AND
COTTON BOWLS. SUCCESS ADDED
UP, GRADUATING AS THE SCHOOL'S
ALL-TIME TOTAL OFFENSE LEADER
WITH 8,290 YARDS.

THE UNIVERSITY OF PITTSBURGH
PRODUCED A TRADING CARD OF
MARINO AS PART OF A 22-CARD
SET OF PITT FOOTBALL GREATS
INCLUDING TONY DORSETT AND
MIKE DITKA. THE CARD ACTUALLY
WAS PRODUCED IN 1989 — FIVE
YEARS AFTER HIS GRADUATION.

The Lions scored 48 unanswered points to make a shambles of Pitt, as the team's dream of another championship went up in smoke. "It was the first time I ever saw Marino lose his cool," Sherrill said. "He became impatient, and lost control of himself for that one afternoon. He was back to being patient Danny the next game in the Sugar Bowl against Georgia. Dan was the picture of patience that day, particularly on that last drive."

With fourth and three on the Georgia 30, with about 30 seconds to play, Marino lofted his 26th completion of the game. The ball fell into the waiting arms of Tom Brown as he crossed the final stripe in an extremely hard-fought 24–20 victory.

"He learned in the stretch between the loss to Penn State and the victory at the Superdome, that a quarterback must be in control of the situation for the entire game," Sherrill said. "It was a lesson he had to learn and he learned it well, putting us in great shape for the season-ending showdown against Georgia."

Four of the men who blocked for Marino at Pitt were fullback Randy McMillan, who played for the Baltimore and Indianapolis Colts, offensive linemen Jim Covert, who played for the Chicago Bears, and two future Washington Redskins, Russ Grimm and Mark May. McMillan, Covert and May were first round choices while Grimm lasted until Round 3. Another Marino blocker was Jim Sweeney, a third-round choice with the New York Jets who is now finishing up his career with the hometown Steelers.

"Marino was a tough, highly focused kid from South Oakland who turned a good Pitt team into a powerhouse," said Sweeney, who also lived part of his youth in Oakland. "Danny came from a down-to-earth family: two sisters and himself with parents who knew how to raise children. They were good, hard-working, God-fearing people, like so many Oaklanders of that time."

MARINO AND HIS ABILITY TO AIR IT OUT BROUGHT A NEW BRAND OF BALL TO THE PANTHERS, WHERE TRADITIONALLY THE POUND-IT-OUT, GROUND GAME HAD BEEN THE FOCUS.

As a writer who spent 35 years covering the Steelers for the Pittsburgh Press, I was hoping they would draft Marino when they had a chance, but when they didn't, and I understood why. At the time, there was no indication that Terry Bradshaw was anywhere near the end of his career, and as backups in case he was, Coach Chuck Noll had two quarterbacks who were rated as "Can't Miss" prospects in Cliff Stoudt and Mark Malone. Both got their chances with the Steelers but neither showed any of the ability Marino possessed.

As draft day approached in 1983, rumors started circulating that Dan Marino was fooling around with drugs. The rumors became more plausible as choice after choice was made without mention of him, but nothing more came of the issue. The Dolphins nabbed Marino with the 27th pick, and haven't looked back since.

MARINO DOMINATED AS A JUNIOR AT PITT, SETTING SCHOOL RECORDS FOR PASSING YARDS (2,876) AND TOUCHDOWNS IN A SEASON (37). HE ALSO EARNED ALL-AMERICA HONORS AND WAS FOURTH IN HEISMAN TROPHY VOTING.

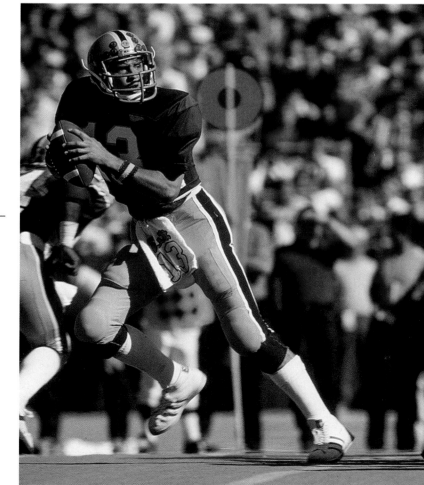

MARINO WORE NO. 13 IN HIGH SCHOOL, AT PITTSBURGH AND WITH THE DOLPHINS. THE ONLY TIME HE WORE A DIFFERENT NUMBER WAS DURING PRACTICE DRILLS.

MARINO'S STATISTICS AT PITT 1979–1982

Year	Att.	Comp.	Pct.	Yds.	TD	Int.
1979	222	130	.586	1,680	10	9
1980	224	116	.518	1,609	15	14
1981	380	226	.595	2,876	37	23
1982	378	221	.584	2,432	17	23
Totals	1,204	693	.576	8,597	79	69

CLASS OF HIS OWN

BY VIC CARUCCI

No, not a single draft that preceded that class, the legendary Quarterback Class of 1983, can compare to its remarkable collection of talent at the most important position in the game. It remains to be seen whether anything that follows, such as the five quarterbacks selected in the first round of the 1999 draft, can produce similar results.

But for now, the group of six first-round QBs in '83 stands alone. And one of its best was the man Don Shula coached for 13 seasons with the Miami Dolphins — Dan Marino. Considering the company he was in, that is saying plenty.

John Elway put together a Hall of Fame career with the Denver Broncos, winning the only two Super Bowls of the class before calling it quits on May 2, 1999. Jim Kelly was the leather-tough warrior who guided the Buffalo Bills to four consecutive Super Bowls before his retirement in 1997. And there were the others: Ken O'Brien of the New York Jets (1983–92) and Philadelphia Eagles (1993), Tony Eason of the New England Patriots (1983–89) and Jets (1989–90), and Todd Blackledge of the Kansas City Chiefs (1983–87) and Pittsburgh Steelers (1988–89).

AFTER SUFFERING A KNEE SPRAIN IN THE FOURTH QUARTER OF A GAME AGAINST THE OILERS, MARINO WAS FORCED TO MISS THE LAST TWO REGULAR-SEASON GAMES OF THE '83 SEASON. HE SHOWED HIS TOUGHNESS BY GETTING BACK ON THE FIELD QUICKLY, WEARING A KNEE BRACE FOR A FIRST-ROUND PLAYOFF GAME AGAINST THE SEATTLE SEAHAWKS.

[35]

LEFT: JOHN ELWAY
BELOW: TODD
BLACKLEDGE

FIVE QUARTERBACKS WERE TAKEN AHEAD OF MARINO IN THE 1983 DRAFT. BUT MARINO IS THE ONLY MEMBER OF THE CLASS STILL ACTIVE. JOHN ELWAY WAS DRAFTED NO. 1 (COLTS) OVERALL BUT WAS TRADED TO THE BRONCOS BEFORE THE START OF THE SEASON. THE CHIEFS TOOK TODD BLACKLEDGE 7TH AND JIM KELLY WAS THE 14TH (BUFFALO BILLS) SELECTION, BUT PLAYED IN THE USFL HIS FIRST TWO SEASONS. TONY EASON WAS THE 15TH (NEW ENGLAND PATRIOTS) QUARTERBACK PICKED AND KEN O'BRIEN WAS TAKEN 24TH (JETS), THREE PICKS BEFORE MARINO WAS SNATCHED UP BY THE DOLPHINS.

LEFT : JIM KELLY

BELOW: TONY EASON

BELOW, LEFT: KEN O'BRIEN

Together all six have thrown for 187,377 yards, or roughly 107 miles. They have started 11 Super Bowls. They have been selected to 23 Pro Bowls. To put that in perspective, the 22 quarterbacks selected in the first rounds of the 15 non-supplemental drafts since 1983 have thrown for 242,420 yards, started in four Super Bowls and been chosen for 13 Pro Bowls.

"That was still a special class," Hall-of-Fame quarterback and Fox Network studio analyst Terry Bradshaw says. "Even before John won a Super Bowl."

Now, only Marino remains active.

It is, perhaps, fitting that he be the last to leave because as unbelievable as it might seem, he was the last to be taken. Elway, from Stanford, was chosen first by Baltimore, then subsequently traded to Denver; Blackledge, from Penn State, was seventh; Kelly, from Miami, was 14th and spent two seasons in the United States Football League before joining the Bills in 1986; Eason, from Illinois, was 15th; O'Brien, from the University of California-Davis, was 24th . . . and then Marino, from Pittsburgh, was 27th, the next-to-last pick of the first round.

The Minnesota Vikings might have gotten one of the all-time steals when they chose wide receiver Randy Moss with the 21st overall pick of the 1998 draft. But what the Dolphins committed by getting Marino with the 27th choice of the 1983 draft was nothing short of grand larceny. How could Marino have slipped so far?

Two reasons. One was fact: He had a sub-par senior season at Pitt, throwing 17 touchdowns against 23 interceptions. The other was a rumor that was never proven: that he had used drugs.

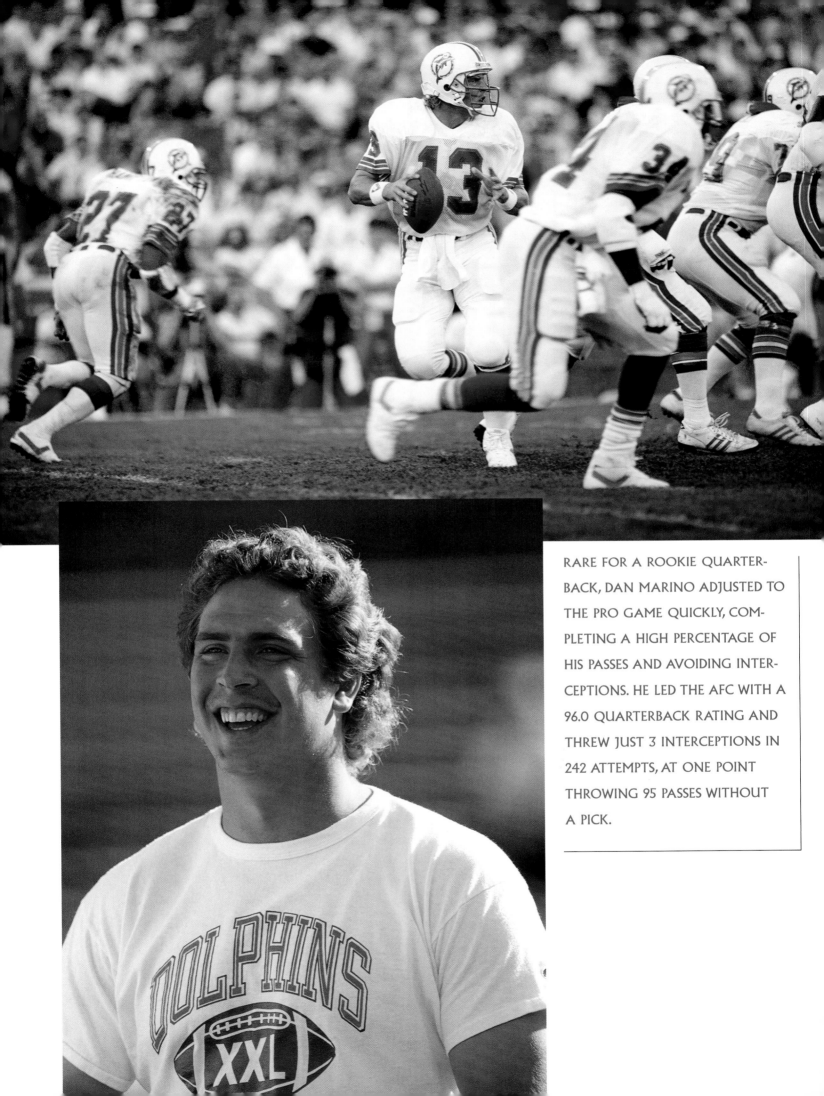

RARE FOR A ROOKIE QUARTER-
BACK, DAN MARINO ADJUSTED TO
THE PRO GAME QUICKLY, COM-
PLETING A HIGH PERCENTAGE OF
HIS PASSES AND AVOIDING INTER-
CEPTIONS. HE LED THE AFC WITH A
96.0 QUARTERBACK RATING AND
THREW JUST 3 INTERCEPTIONS IN
242 ATTEMPTS, AT ONE POINT
THROWING 95 PASSES WITHOUT
A PICK.

WANT TO WISH A FRIEND HAPPY BIRTHDAY — MARINO STYLE? YOU CAN SEND A DAN MARINO GREETING CARD MADE BY THE BERNIE KOSAR CARD COMPANY.

ALBEIT IT A LOSS, MARINO WAS STUNNING IN HIS FIRST PROFESSIONAL START VERSUS THE BUFFALO BILLS. HE COMPLETED 19 OF 29 PASSES FOR 322 YARDS AND THREE TOUCHDOWNS IN A 38–35 OVERTIME LOSS. AFTER THE GAME DON SHULA PROMISED, "YOU'LL SEE MORE OF THAT FROM MARINO. HE'S CAPABLE OF MAKING THE BIG PLAYS."

Chuck Noll, the Steelers' coach at the time, says he and other league decision-makers were scared off by the rumor — apparently originated in a suburban Pittsburgh newspaper — because "this was a time when no one (in the NFL) knew anything about drugs at all."

"The fact that he didn't score well on the Wunderlich IQ test also helped scare some teams," recalls noted draftnik Joel Buchsbaum." The reason he struggled as a senior was that he developed a flaw in his throwing motion. As a result, his release point was off, causing his throws to lack accuracy and zip. Instead of zipping balls between two defenders, Marino's ball was hanging up or going over receivers' heads and very often wound up in the defenders' hands.

MARINO'S FIRST PLAY AS AN NFL QUARTERBACK WASN'T FLASHY, BUT IT GOT THE JOB DONE. HE THREW A SIDELINE COMPLETION TO WIDE RECEIVER MARK DUPER FOR NINE YARDS. THAT PASS MARKED THE FIRST OF 492 COMPLETIONS MARINO THREW TO CLAYTON OVER HIS CAREER.

"However, he corrected the flaw and looked sharp in the Hula and Senior bowls (winning Most Valuable Player honors in both), but scouts couldn't forget that senior season—and the 1983 draft contained more great players than any draft in NFL history."

Shula put no stock in the rumor about drug use. He also took Marino's entire collegiate career into account, not just his senior year, along with his impressive post-season performances. But he never expected to have a chance to draft him. So when the Los Angeles Raiders used the 26th pick to select offensive tackle Don Mosebar, Shula promptly grabbed Marino.

"It didn't bother me at all," Marino says of his draft position.

Shula loved Marino's quick release, quick feet, awareness and field presence. They were qualities he knew the Dolphins desperately needed at quarterback six games into the '83 season after David Woodley, who had led them to the Super Bowl in 1982, had faltered.

"We had three games in which we couldn't make a first down, couldn't complete a pass. We were struggling," Shula says. "So, knowing that Marino had been looking good and had that quick release, I just decided to give him the opportunity."

The opportunity came against the Buffalo Bills on Oct. 9, 1983. The Dolphins lost in overtime, 38–35, but Marino established himself as a force, completing 19 of 29 passes for 322 yards and three touchdowns, while throwing two interceptions.

In the same game, Shula replaced veteran wide receiver Duriel Harris with a diminutive second-year player named Mark Duper, who proceeded to catch seven passes for 202 yards and two TDs. Marino-to-Duper went on to become one of the most electrifying passing combinations in the NFL that year and beyond.

"I like catching the ball from Dan because with him throwing, I can be more flexible with my routes," Duper said at the time. "Dan can just hang the ball up and let me run under it."

In nine starts, Marino led the Dolphins to an 8-1 record and a playoff berth.

Marino wound up suffering a sprained left knee on a fourth-quarter scramble against Houston on Dec. 4. That caused him to miss the final two games of the regular season. Wearing a knee brace, he returned to action to face Seattle in the playoffs. Marino was 15-of-25 for 193 yards and two TDs, and threw two interceptions in the Dolphins' 27–20 loss. He underwent arthroscopic surgery on the knee on Jan. 6, 1984.

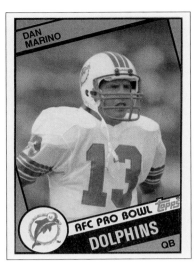

HIS TRUE ROOKIE CARD AND FIRST NFL TRADING CARD, THE 1994 TOPPS DAN MARINO IS CONSIDERED ONE OF THE TOP FOOTBALL CARDS — EVER. THE ENTIRE SET WAS FULL OF ROOKIE CARDS INCLUDING OTHER ALL-EVERYTHING PLAYERS: JOHN ELWAY, ERIC DICKERSON, ROGER CRAIG AND HOWIE LONG. THE OTHER FOOTBALL CARD SET THAT YEAR WAS THE 1984 TOPPS USFL SET. THAT SET ALSO WAS STOCKED, INCLUDING THE ROOKIE CARDS OF JIM KELLY, STEVE YOUNG, REGGIE WHITE AND HERSCHEL WALKER.

Marino finished his rookie season as the AFC passing champion
with 175 completions in 296 attempts for 2,210 yards and 20 TDs,
while throwing six interceptions. He was selected to start in the Pro
Bowl ahead of San Diego's Dan Fouts. Although he couldn't play in
the game because of the knee surgery, that selection clearly helped ease
whatever pain he might have felt from the selection that had brought
him into the league.

"To be picked ahead of him (for the Pro Bowl)," Marino said,
"that's a hell of an honor."

1983 NFL DRAFT
FIRST ROUND

1.	BALTIMORE COLTS	JOHN ELWAY	QB	STANFORD
2.	LOS ANGELES RAMS	ERIC DICKERSON	RB	SMU
3.	SEATTLE SEAHAWKS	CURT WARNER	RB	PENN STATE
4.	DENVER BRONCOS	CHRIS HINTON	OL	NORTHWESTERN
5.	SAN DIEGO CHARGERS	BILLY RAY SMITH	LB	ARKANSAS
6.	CHICAGO BEARS	JIMBO COVERT	OL	PITTSBURGH
7.	KANSAS CITY CHIEFS	TODD BLACKLEDGE	QB	PENN STATE
8.	PHILADELPHIA EAGLES	MICHAEL HADDIX	RB	MISSISSIPPI STATE
9.	HOUSTON OILERS	BRUCE MATHEWS	OL	USC
10.	NEW YORK GIANTS	TERRY KINARD	DB	CLEMSON
11.	GREEN BAY PACKERS	TIM LEWIS	CB	PITTSBURGH
12.	BUFFALO BILLS	TONY HUNTER	TE	NOTRE DAME
13.	DETROIT LIONS	JAMES JONES	FB	FLORIDA
14.	BUFFALO BILLS	JIM KELLY	QB	MIAMI
15.	NEW ENGLAND PATRIOTS	TONY EASON	QB	ILLINOIS
16.	ATLANTA FALCONS	MIKE PITTS	DE	ALABAMA
17.	ST. LOUIS CARDINALS	LEONARD SMITH	CB	MCNEESE STATE
18.	CHICAGO BEARS	WILLIE GAULT	WR	TENNESSEE
19.	MINNESOTA VIKINGS	JOEY BROWNER	DB	USC
20.	SAN DIEGO CHARGERS	GARY ANDERSON	RB	ARKANSAS
21.	PITTSBURGH STEELERS	GABRIEL RIVERA	DT	TEXAS TECH
22.	SAN DIEGO CHARGERS	GILL BYRD	CB	SAN JOSE STATE
23.	DALLAS COWBOYS	JIM JEFFCOAT	DE	ARIZONA STATE
24.	NEW YORK JETS	KEN O'BRIEN	QB	CALIFORNIA-DAVIS
25.	CINCINNATI BENGALS	DAVE RIMINGTON	C	NEBRASKA
26.	LOS ANGELES RAIDERS	DON MOSEBAR	OL	USC
27.	MIAMI DOLPHINS	DAN MARINO	QB	PITTSBURGH
28.	WASHINGTON REDSKINS	DARRELL GREEN	CB	TEXAS A&I

SUPER SOPHOMORE

BY DON SHULA
AS TOLD TO KEVIN KAMINSKI

To say that Dan Marino caught the entire NFL off guard in 1984 is a major understatement. Who could have possibly envisioned a second-year quarterback setting single-season league records for yards and touchdowns — marks which still stand today?

It's even more remarkable when one considers that the Miami Dolphins entered the previous year's draft ready to take a defensive lineman. Oh, we knew Marino was something special. We had Dan ranked as the No. 2 quarterback that year, right behind John Elway. But what were the odds that someone that talented would be there with the 27th overall selection?

Incredibly, as our pick drew closer, Marino was still on the board. How? Well, though he enjoyed an outstanding junior year at the University of Pittsburgh, Marino didn't have the same success his senior season. Because of that, there were some rumors about off-the-field activities that probably hurt his standing in the draft.

But when it looked like we had a chance to land Marino, I switched gears. The defensive lineman could wait. I immediately called Dan's college coach, Foge Fazio, and asked him what was happening. Foge couldn't believe it either. He said Marino was a wonderful kid,

IN THE OPENING GAME OF THE 1984 SEASON MARINO DRILLED THE WASHINGTON REDSKINS, 35–17, COMPLETING 21 OF 28 PASSES FOR 311 YARDS, FIVE TOUCHDOWNS AND NO INTERCEPTIONS. MARINO CONTINUED TO HAVE THE MOST PROLIFIC SEASON A QUARTERBACK HAS EVER HAD IN THE NFL, SETTING SINGLE-SEASON RECORDS FOR TOUCHDOWN PASSES (48) AND PASSING YARDS (5,084).

FOR 13 YEARS DAN MARINO KNEW ONLY ONE COACH, DON SHULA. THEIR RELATIONSHIP WAS THE SECOND LONGEST QUARTERBACK-COACH COMBINATION IN NFL HISTORY. MARINO HAD GREAT SUCCESS UNDER SHULA WITH 116 WINS, THE MOST VICTORIES BY A QUARTERBACK UNDER ONE COACH IN NFL HISTORY.

IN THE MIDST OF AN 11-GAME WINNING STREAK TO OPEN THE '84 SEASON, MARINO THREW FOR 316 YARDS AND FOUR TOUCHDOWN PASSES AGAINST NEW ENGLAND, INCLUDING A 15-YARD TD PASS TO MARK CLAYTON.

MARK CLAYTON CAUGHT 538 PASSES FOR 8,468 YARDS FROM MARINO FOR HIS CAREER. MARINO WOULD THROW DEEP AND OFTEN TO THE RECEIVER, ALLOWING HIM TO RACK UP 79 TOUCHDOWN PASSES, MAKING THEM THE NO. 2 ALL-TIME NFL SCORING COMBINATION.

came from a great family and gave him every possible recommendation. That was enough for me. Time and again, for the duration of my coaching career, Marino would reward that faith.

From the moment Dan stepped on the field at our first minicamp, we knew it was only a matter of time before he ran the offense. Where then-starter David Woodley was an athlete trying to play quarterback, Marino was a quarterback in every sense of the word. Even as a rookie, his timing, his reads, and his command of the offense proved uncanny.

When I finally made the move and started Dan the fifth game of his first year, he immediately breathed life into our offense. (He would complete nearly 60 percent of his passes for 20 touchdowns and just six interceptions to earn Rookie of the Year honors.)

So entering the 1984 season, we decided to open the offense up. Why not utilize this kid's amazing gifts? As a coach, I always understood what I had to work with. I then tried to put players in a position to capitalize on their skills. I did it with Johnny Unitas and Earl Morrall at Baltimore, and with Bob Griese and Morrall at Miami.

Given Marino's particular skills, we weren't about to grind it out. So after having success for years with a ground-oriented attack, the Dolphins began airing it out.

In the 1984 season opener at Washington, Marino completed 21 of 28 for 311 yards with five touchdowns, including a 74-yarder to Mark Duper that sent us on our way to a 35–17 victory. Few teams were ever consistent with the deep ball over the course of a season, especially with a second-year quarterback behind center. So opponents, early on, continued to play us with tight coverages and loads of pressure.

Bad move. Not only could Marino sidestep the rush like a veteran, he had one of the quickest releases I had ever seen. With all the blitzing early in the season, we were getting great one-on-one matchups at wide receiver with Duper and Mark Clayton. Remember, Clayton and Duper were also relative unknowns at that time. Defenses were stunned that our wideouts could get deep and make plays. (By season's end, Dan would complete 12 touchdown passes of 30 yards or better, with all but two going to Clayton or Duper.)

Typically, the run sets up the pass. But that year, it was just the opposite. As the season wore on, and defenses pulled back into coverage instead of blitzing, we saw more three-man rushes. If you weren't going to get to Marino anyway, why not put eight bodies in the secondary? So defenses backed off, tried to take away the bomb, and surrendered the run and short passes. The hope was that, somewhere along the line, we would make a mistake.

But Marino was just too good. He recognized the soft coverages, took what the defense allowed, and still hit for the big play.

By the following season, after teams had a year to study us,

PRESIDENTS AND DICTATORS AREN'T THE ONLY ONES WITH THEIR LIKENESSES ON COINS. MARINO'S MUG IS USED ON FOOTBALL COINS MADE BY PINNACLE BRANDS AS PART OF THE 1997 AND 1998 PINNACLE MINT COLLECTION SET.

MARINO TO MARK DUPER FORMED THE FIFTH BEST SCORING COMBINATION IN NFL HISTORY WITH 55 TOUCHDOWN CATCHES. MARINO'S 48 TOUCHDOWNS FOR THE 1984 SEASON WERE MORE TDs THAN 22 OF MIAMI'S OTHER 23 QUARTERBACKS HAVE THROWN IN THEIR DOLPHINS CAREERS.

MARINO THREW 492 COMPLE-
TIONS FOR 8,475 YARDS TO
MARK DUPER FOR HIS CAREER. IN
HIS RECORD-BREAKING SEASON,
MARINO THREW FOR 400 YARDS
FIVE TIMES, 300 YARDS SIX TIMES
AND SHATTERED NEARLY EVERY
DOLPHINS' SEASON RECORD.

defenses began to slow us down. In 1984, however, our offense seemed unstoppable. That season we won our first 11 games, most of them rather easily. We were just destroying teams. We blitzed the Colts (44–7) and crushed Pittsburgh (31–7). Dan threw for 429 yards and three scores in a 36–28 win over St. Louis; he had four touchdowns in a victory at New England.

But at San Diego, we met with disappointment for the first time. Marino threw for 338 yards, but we blew a fourth-quarter lead and eventually lost 34–28 in overtime. Still, talk about some fireworks. You had San Diego's Dan Fouts on one side and Marino lighting it up on the other side. That matchup would still excite people today.

We finished the regular season 14–2. We were having so much fun that year moving the ball—we used flea flickers, we ran play-action in third-and-1 and fourth-and-1 situations — and doing anything to take advantage of Dan's talent. Everything clicked. The offensive line surrendered only 13 sacks. Tony Nathan was a tremendous weapon for us out of the backfield. Nat Moore excelled in our three-wide sets, exploiting secondaries underneath.

But as good as things were going, I felt they could get even better. And after knocking off Seattle in our opening playoff game, that's exactly what happened. Marino and our record-setting offense put it all together in the AFC Championship against the Steelers. From the opening kickoff, we came out wide open, daring Pittsburgh to cover us. They couldn't do it.

Marino threw for 421 yards and four touchdowns. Duper had five receptions for 148 yards and two long touchdowns. We even rushed

IN SUPER BOWL XIX, MARINO COMPLETED 29 OF 50 PASSES FOR 318 YARDS AND ONE TOUCH-DOWN IN THE LOSS TO THE SAN FRANCISCO 49ERS. BUT THE LOSS DIDN'T SEEM TO HURT HIS POPU-LARITY; MARINO WAS NAMED IN A NATIONWIDE POLL CONDUCTED BY CBS AND *THE NEW YORK TIMES* AS THE MOST POPULAR FOOTBALL PLAYER IN AMERICA.

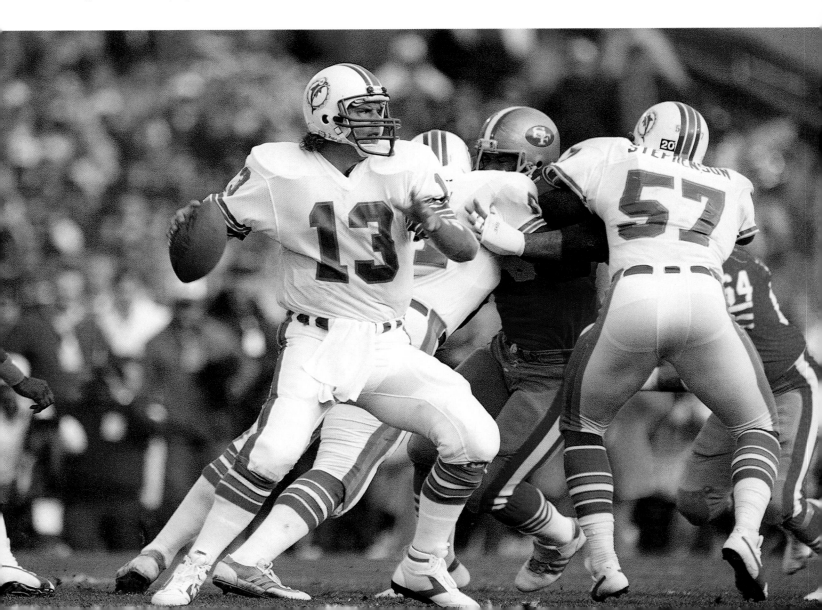

RELIVING THE DREAM

In his sophomore NFL season, Dan Marino announced his presence by shattering NFL records for touchdowns (48) and yards passing (5,048) and leading the Dolphins to Super Bowl XIX. The following is a game-by-game breakdown of Marino's 1984 season.

Date	Opponent	Yds	TD	W/L	Score
9/2	at Washington	311	5	W	35–17
	Touchdowns:	26 yards to Mark Duper			
		74 yards to Duper			
		6 yards to Jim Jensen			
		9 yards to Mark Clayton			
		11 yards to Jensen			
9/9	New England	234	2	W	28–7
	Touchdowns:	38 yards to Clayton			
		15 yards to Clayton			
9/17	at Buffalo	296	3	W	21–17
	Touchdowns:	11 yards to Duper			
		12 yards to Clayton			
		1 yard to Nat Moore			
9/23	Indianapolis	257	2	W	44–7
	Touchdowns:	80 yards to Duper			
		5 yards to Duper			
9/30	at St. Louis	429	3	W	36–28
	Touchdowns:	26 yards to Joe Rose			
		29 yards to Clayton			
		23 yards to Tony Nathan			
10/7	at Pittsburgh	226	2	W	31–7
	Touchdowns:	3 yards to Bruce Hardy			
		34 yards to Rose			

THE 1997 DONRUSS PREFERRED FOOTBALL TRADING CARDS WERE PRODUCED IN SMALL TINS THAT WERE SOLD IN TIN BOXES. THE BOXES COULD BE USED TO STORE TRADING CARDS, BUT WOULDN'T COME CLOSE TO HOLDING THE MORE THAN 2,250 TRADING CARDS THAT HAVE BEEN PRODUCED OF MARINO.

Date	Opponent	Yds	TD	W/L	Score
10/14	Houston	321	3	W	28–10
	Touchdowns:	27 yards to Clayton			
		17 yards to Duper			
		32 yards to Moore			
10/21	at New England	316	4	W	44–24
	Touchdowns:	19 yards to Moore			
		4 yards to Dan Johnson			
		15 yards to Clayton			
		15 yards to Moore			
10/28	Buffalo	282	3	W	38–7
	Touchdowns:	7 yards to Clayton			
		10 yards to Johnson			
		65 yards to Clayton			
11/4	at N.Y. Jets	422	2	W	31–17
	Touchdowns:	37 yards to Moore			
		47 yards to Clayton			
11/11	Philadelphia	246	1	W	24–23
	Touchdown:	11 yards to Nathan			
11/18	at San Diego	338	2	L	28–34 (OT)
	Touchdowns:	12 yards to Clayton			
		4 yards to Woody Bennett			
11/26	N.Y. Jets	192	4	W	28–17
	Touchdowns:	5 yards to Clayton			
		1 yard to Hardy			
		7 yards to Johnson			
		12 yards to Hardy			
12/2	L.A. Raiders	470	4	L	34–45
	Touchdowns:	4 yards to Jimmy Cefalo			
		64 yards to Clayton			
		11 yards to Clayton			
		9 yards to Duper			

Date	Opponent	Yds	TD	W/L	Score
12/9	at Indianapolis	404	4	W	35–17
	Touchdowns:	2 yards to Moore			
		2 yards to Hardy			
		25 yards to Cefalo			
		7 yards to Clayton			
12/17	Dallas	340	4	W	28–21
	Touchdowns:	41 yards to Clayton			
		3 yards to Hardy			
		39 yards to Clayton			
		83 yards to Clayton			
Regular-Season Totals		5,084	48		14–2

Regular-Season Touchdowns Receiving (No.-yards): Clayton (18-526), Duper (7-222), Moore (6-106), Hardy (5-21), Johnson (3-21), Rose (2-60), Nathan (2-34), Cefalo (2-29), Jensen (2-17), Bennett (1-4).

WHO NEEDS A TEDDY BEAR WHEN YOU CAN HAVE A DAN MARINO DOLL? MADE BY STARTING LINEUP, THE 1998 12-INCH DOLL HAS A GREAT DEAL OF DETAIL INCLUDING A TOWEL TUCKED IN THE WAISTBAND AND A DOLPHINS HELMET WITH FACEMASK.

PLAYOFF STATISTICS

12/29	Seattle	262	3	W	31–10
	Touchdowns:	26 yards to Clayton			
		34 yards to Cefalo			
		3 yards to Hardy			
1/6	Pittsburgh	421	4	W	45–28
	Touchdowns:	40 yards to Clayton			
		41 yards to Duper			
		36 yards to Duper			
		6 yards to Moore			
1/20	San Francisco	318	1	L	16–38
	Touchdowns:	2 yards to Johnson			

TOOLS OF THE TRADE

BY PHIL SIMMS
AS TOLD TO VIC CARUCCI

The things that make Dan Marino a great quarterback are physical ability along with extreme confidence. I don't know what came first. I think his physical ability was so great, that it gave him extreme confidence and arrogance. You put those together, and you've got a guy who thinks he's unstoppable.

I'm a lot older than Dan, about seven years older, but I've learned a lot just from sitting around and talking with him while playing golf and so forth during the offseason. I remember once, when we were having a beer after we had played a round of golf, I said to him, "You know, you are a cocky SOB."

He said, "Damn right, I am."

And I realized that that's one of his greatest traits. He never throws an incompletion or an interception where there was something wrong on his part. It's a case of, "You ran a wrong route ... Protect me longer ... Come on, catch it!" That could be a really negative thing toward your teammates, but Dan's got a way about him where, somehow, it has worked extremely well. It's a great, great thing.

THE MOST PROLIFIC PASSER IN NFL HISTORY, MARINO HOLDS NEARLY EVERY SIGNIFICANT LEAGUE PASSING RECORD. HIS QUICK RELEASE, STRONG ARM, FIELD VISION AND INSTINCTS COMBINE TO MAKE HIM THE PROTOTYPICAL PASSER.

NOW A TV COMMENTATOR FOR NBC, PHIL SIMMS KNOWS SOMETHING
ABOUT QUARTERBACKING. HE PLAYED FOR THE NEW YORK GIANTS FROM
1979–1993 AND LED THEM TO A VICTORY IN SUPER BOWL XXI. IN THE 39–20
WIN OVER DENVER, SIMMS WAS 22 FOR 25 FOR 268 YARDS AND 3 TDs. HE
ALSO HOLDS THE GIANTS CAREER RECORDS FOR PASSING YARDS (33,462)
AND TOUCHDOWN PASSES (199).

"ONE DAY IN PRACTICE, DAN WAS SCRAMBLING AND HE FIRED THIS
SHOVEL PASS," RECALLED FORMER DOLPHINS RECEIVER, MARK INGRAM. "IT
HITS (KEITH JACKSON) IN THE SHOULDER PADS AND MAKES SUCH A LOUD
SOUND, YOU'RE WONDERING HOW ANYONE COULD THROW THAT HARD."

MARINO IS ONE OF THE BEST IN THE BUSINESS WHEN IT COMES TO READ-ING A DEFENSE. THAT ABILITY ALONG WITH HIS QUICK RELEASE AND NIM-BLE FEET HAS ENABLED HIM TO AVOID SACKS OVER HIS CAREER. FOR THE FIRST EIGHT SEASONS OF MARINO'S CAREER THE DOLPHINS ALLOWED THE FEWEST SACKS IN THE NFL (1983–1990).

His throwing style is unique. It has changed over the years. When he came into the league, he was a different-looking athlete with probably a longer throwing motion. He was a harder, longer thrower at the time. Since then, because of injuries and wear and tear over the course of time, he has adjusted and streamlined his throwing motion, which has always been productive.

I'm not sure the changes have always been for the better, but athletes do what their bodies tell them to do. Ten years later, I think we all perceive ourselves as still the same athlete. But when we see a game film of ourselves from 10 years ago, we say, "Holy, shoot! I could really run back then … I was really loose."

You don't even realize how much your game changes through the years. Dan's mechanics are probably as good as anyone's you'll ever see. People always talk about his quick release, but there are other things such as his position when he gets ready to throw and his footwork in the pocket. The great thing is that he has no wasted motion. He has a very extended follow-through, which is how he creates the power to throw it. He throws with no inhibitions, he throws with confidence, and he does get rid of it so quickly.

His footwork in the pocket is a clinic. You could make a reel off of Dan Marino, and if you could show it to everybody that ever plays the quarterback position, you could say, "That is what mobility is in professional football." He is maybe the best that's ever played at buying time in the pocket — at feeling and sensing and hopping around and making throws.

ANYTHING SIGNED BY DAN MARINO IS AN INSTANT COLLECTIBLE, BUT AN AUTHENTIC, LEATHER NFL FOOTBALL AUTOGRAPHED BY THE MIAMI DOLPHIN IS A CENTERPIECE OF NEARLY ANY COLLECTION.

He doesn't scramble in the classic sense of the word; he hops. But the thing about his hopping is that he's always in position to throw. As he hops, he keeps everything in perfect position, and that's why he can still throw it. Most guys who are runners, turn and get into a running position, and when they do that they're beat. They can't throw it down the field anymore. So they have to continue to run or really run around a lot to gather themselves up again to throw the football.

I would take Dan Marino's mobility over that of a Kordell Stewart or those types of scramblers. His ability to feel and sense things and move around and buy the extra time is always overlooked. How many times has Dan Marino moved in the pocket and made a throw that ended up in a big play? It's safe to say four to five times every single game of his whole career.

In his early years in the league, he had a tremendous arm. To throw the ball and to be so effective for so long, you have to have a great arm when you come into the league. Sixteen years later, his arm strength is still way above average for the NFL. He's not a great downfield thrower anymore, as far as the long post or deep, down the sideline. But as far as what I would call long-range power throws, he's still very good.

Early on, and especially in 1984, Dan was like Brett Favre in these past three or four years: He just reared back and threw it with complete abandon and confidence. That probably explains his success as a player his whole career anyway. Then you took a guy who was

YOU'LL NEED A CAN OPENER TO ACCESS A PACK OF 1997 PINNACLE INSIDE FOOTBALL TRADING CARDS. THE MARINO CAN IS ONE OF 28 IN THE SET, EACH HOLDING 10 NFL TRADING CARDS.

probably athletically at the top of his game and you put him in great weather. And don't underestimate Miami as a great place to throw the football. It's warm, there's humidity in the air ... it is absolutely conducive to throwing the football. Yes, you'll get a little breeze every once in a while, but every quarterback in the league would take that to have the other conditions. Then you put him behind an offensive line that was second to none and give him playmakers. Everything was there for him to put up the numbers. You cannot do what he did unless there are really dynamic players with you, and he had them.

IT'S SAID THAT A STRONG GROUND GAME CAN OPEN THINGS UP FOR THE PASS, BUT FOR MOST OF MARINO'S CAREER IN MIAMI HE'S BEEN A ONE-MAN SHOW. NOW WITH JIMMY JOHNSON'S EMPHASIS ON A RUNNING GAME, THERE IS LESS PRESSURE ON MARINO TO CARRY THE TEAM EVERY GAME.

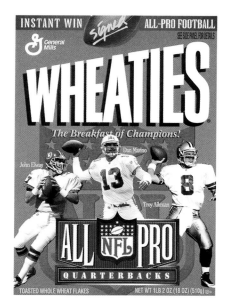

THE ULTIMATE FOR ANY ATHLETE IS APPEARING ON THE FRONT OF A WHEATIES BOX. THE ALL-PRO QUARTERBACKS WHEATIES BOX INCLUDED FUTURE HALL-OF-FAME QUARTERBACKS JOHN ELWAY, TROY AIKMAN AND DAN MARINO. FOR MARINO IT WAS HIS SECOND APPEARANCE ON THE FRONT OF A WHEATIES BOX.

When Dan Marino was having those great years earlier in his career, he was not a great reader of defenses, mainly because he was young. He just relied on his physical talent and the talent around him, and the two of them together were so great, they just overcame everything. But over the years, as he has gained experience, he has become an excellent reader of defenses.

As I've done Dolphins' games and watched a lot of films over the past couple of years, I've noticed that the thing that Dan does so well is that he doesn't have to wait for the play to develop. He just takes what's there right now. There are so many things involved in being a good reader of a defense. I would say the first thing is really knowing your offense inside out. Probably the second thing is never having any questions or doubts about your physical abilities. Extreme arrogance and confidence are important, and Dan's got plenty of both. And the last thing is actually seeing the defense itself and reacting to it.

His play alone makes him an outstanding leader. When you're such a dynamic player, it gives you tremendous respect and a following from the team — the owner, coaches, players, everyone. And he carries himself like a leader.

I haven't seen all of the great quarterbacks who have played the game — the Sid Luckmans, the Bobby Lanes, the Otto Grahams. But from my modern perspective, since I was a kid to right now, he would be one of the top three, along with John Elway and Brett Favre.

How do you stop Dan Marino? Slap yourself and wake up. Because it ain't gonna happen.

DAN MARINO'S NFL RECORDS
1983–1998

Most Career Passing Attempts	7,989
Most Career Passing Completions	4,763
Most Career Passing Yards	58,913
Most Career Touchdown Passes	408
Most Yards Gained in a Season	5,084
Highest Rookie-Season Pass Rating	96.0
Highest Rookie-Season Completion Percentage	58.45%
Most Touchdown Passes in a Season	48
Most Career Games With 400 or More Yards Passing	13
Most Games with 400 or More Yards Passing in a Season	4
Most Career Games with 300 or More Yards Passing	60
Most Seasons with 3,000 or More Yards Passing	13
Most Consecutive Seasons with 3,000 or More Yards Passing	9
Most Career Games with Four or More Touchdown Passes	21
Most Games with Four or More Touchdown Passes in a Season	6
Most Consecutive Games with Four or More Touchdown Passes	4
Lowest Percentage of Passes Intercepted in a Rookie Season	2.03%
Most Seasons Leading the League in Passing Attempts	5
Most Seasons Leading the League in Passing Completions	6
Most Seasons with 40 or More Touchdown Passes	2
Most Seasons with 20 or More Touchdown Passes	13
Most Consecutive Seasons with 20 or More Touchdown Passes	10
100 Touchdown Passes in Fewest Number of Games to Start Career	44 games
200 Touchdown Passes in Fewest Number of Games to Start Career	89 games
300 Touchdown Passes in Fewest Number of Games to Start Career	157 games

Tied Records:

Most Seasons Leading the League in Yards Gained	5
Most Consecutive Seasons Leading the League in Completions	3
Most Consecutive Games with 400 or More Yards Passing	2
Most Consecutive Seasons with 4,000 or More Yards Passing	3
Most Games with 300 or More Yards Passing in a Season	9

ON THE SIDELINES

BY JASON COLE

The greatest time to be around Dan Marino isn't always on game day. Often it's those moments away from the field when he is surrounded by just a few people, perhaps a couple of fellow parents. Parents who have a struggling or dying child they're trying their best to care for.

That's when Marino, who was named the NFL Man of the Year for 1998 and is a regular participant in the Make-A-Wish Foundation, is smiling the broadest, creating an electric atmosphere that only the grandest of heroes can manage. He will loft a few gentle passes to a child, staying there until some healing, albeit temporary, is done.

It is at these times that Marino is at his understated best. He is not a man who likes to be out front with his life away from the field. When asked years ago if he was interested in doing an autobiography, Marino shook off the request with a grin.

"Nah, I think I'll just keep it private. Kinda like Bobby DeNiro," Marino said, referring to his favorite actor. There was another time when Marino was asked by a reporter to talk about adoption. Marino and his wife, Claire, adopted a 2-year-old daughter from China in 1998.

Marino said, "Sure, whatever you want to know, I'll talk to you." When the reporter asked if he could set up a photo of the Marinos with their new child, Marino changed his tune.

IN THE ANNUAL NFL QUARTER-BACK CHALLENGE, THE LEAGUE'S TOP FIELD GENERALS COMPETE IN SKILL-TESTING EVENTS. MARINO ENJOYS BATTLING IN THE QB CHALLENGE, ESPECIALLY WHEN IT'S HELD IN HAWAII. HE HAS WON THE CONTEST BOTH TIMES IT HAS BEEN HELD IN THE ALOHA STATE.

MARINO DIDN'T HAVE TO STUDY TOO MUCH FOR HIS PART IN THE MOVIE, *ACE VENTURA: PET DETECTIVE*. HE PLAYED HIMSELF IN THE JIM CARREY COMEDY. MARINO ALSO APPEARED IN THE MUSIC VIDEO FOR THE HOOTIE AND THE BLOWFISH SONG, *ONLY WANNA BE WITH YOU*. "DAN IS LIKE THE FRANK SINATRA OF MIAMI," SAID DARIUS RUCKER, LEAD SINGER OF HOOTIE AND THE BLOWFISH. "HE'S THE MAN."

STOP IN FOR A BURGER SOMETIME AT DAN MARINO'S TOWN TAVERN IN ORLANDO, FLA. MARINO, A SILENT PARTNER IN THE RESTAURANT, HAS STOCKED THE EATERY WITH HIS MEMORABILIA. YOU CAN EVEN PICK UP A NICE GREEN KOOZIE IN THE GIFT SHOP ON YOUR WAY OUT.

"Oh, you want to do a story," Marino said, obviously not understanding the original request. "No, I think we'll just keep it in the family."

But with children in need, Marino is an open book. Reared in a Pittsburgh neighborhood that was teeming with children, Marino has a soft spot for kids and family. His father, Dan Sr., is a regular at practice, and his parents live nearby in South Florida. The grandparents do most of the babysitting.

"Hey, that's how he was raised," Dan Sr. says. "In our neighborhood, everybody took care of everybody else's kids. If you disobeyed somebody else's mom and dad, you were going to hear about it later, because they'd call your parents."

AS ONE OF THE BETTER AUTO-GRAPH SIGNERS IN THE NFL, MARINO TAKES THE TIME TO SIGN NEATLY AND IN THE BEST PLACE ON EACH ITEM. AND WHEN IT COME TO KIDS WHO WANT AUTO-GRAPHS, HE'S A BIG SOFTIE: HE HAS FIVE CHILDREN OF HIS OWN.

AS ONE OF THE MOST POPULAR PLAYERS IN THE NFL, MARINO IS OFTEN ASKED TO APPEAR IN TELEVISION COMMERCIALS AS A SPOKESMAN FOR DIFFERENT PRODUCTS AND SERVICES. BUT HE ALSO HAS HIS OWN ENTERPRISES, INCLUDING CO-OWNERSHIP, ALONG WITH BILL ELLIOTT, OF THE FIRSTPLUS FINANCIAL NASCAR RACE CAR.

A 6-HANDICAP GOLFER, MARINO TEAMED WITH GOLF PRO DAN POHL TO WIN THE AT&T PEBBLE BEACH NATIONAL PRO-AM IN 1988. BUT SOME OF HIS BEST DAYS ON THE LINKS HAVE BEEN WITH HIS KIDS.

HIS SECOND OLDEST CHILD, MICHAEL, SUFFERS FROM AUTISM, A LIFE-
LONG DEVELOPMENT DISABILITY THAT AFFECTS THE FUNCTIONING OF
THE BRAIN. MARINO HAS ALWAYS SUPPORTED CHILDREN'S CHARITIES OF
ALL KINDS, BUT NOW CHAMPIONS A MORE PERSONAL CAUSE.

MARINO WOULD TELL YOU THAT FOOTBALL IS HIS JOB AND HIS FAMILY
IS HIS LIFE. HE HAS THREE SONS (DANIEL, MICHAEL AND JOSEPH) AND
TWO DAUGHTERS (ALEXANDRA AND NIKI). HE AND HIS WIFE ADOPTED
NIKI SINCE THIS FAMILY PHOTO. HIS DEVOTION HAS ALSO BEEN
DIRECTED TOWARD HIS COMMUNITY; HE ESTABLISHED THE DAN MARINO
FOUNDATION, WHICH HELPS MANY SOUTH FLORIDA CHARITIES.

Now, Marino lends a similar hand to other parents in need.

"You're talking about Dan spreading his magic dust," says Nancy Strom, president of the Make-A-Wish Foundation of South Florida. She gets numerous requests from families with terminally ill children who want to meet Marino.

"Sometimes it's mind-boggling that a child's biggest wish would be to come to a Dolphins game and meet me," Marino says. "Although it can be tough emotionally because of their situation, it's also satisfying for me to see them happy and smiling."

Marino is an open checkbook as well. His fund raising through the Dan Marino Foundation helped build a center in Weston, Fla., that also bears his name. It's an offshoot of the Miami Children's Hospital. Beyond that, he uses his celebrity status to help bring attention to other people and their disabled children.

Marino and his wife have five children. When the second oldest, Michael, was 2, he was diagnosed with mild autism. Now 11, Michael attends the same classes as most other children his age.

The Marinos used to fly from coast to coast looking for the best doctors. After dealing with Michael's illness, Dan and Claire decided to do something for others, so they helped build the wing of the hospital.

"We saw this hospital — putting the kind of doctors we needed in one place — as a way to help some people who are going through the same things we did," Marino says.

"Having five kids, some of the things you go through as a dad — as any dad does — makes you wish some things were better. Michael has had some problems. He's doing incredible now. He's mainstreamed [in school]."

Marino's openness about his son's problems was an inspiration for others. "I've had a lot of families come up to me and say they're only here because Dan Marino came out in the open about his child and

talked about it," says Dr. Roberto Tuchman, executive director of the Miami Children's Hospital and one of Michael's doctors. "There's a lot of stigma attached to this, especially among fathers, like somehow they're to blame for their children's problems. He led the way for a lot of other dads."

Beyond fund raising on the local level, Marino has campaigned for funding on a grander scale. In 1997, he went to the Florida state capitol in Tallahassee to ask for money to help children with autism.

Still, Marino can joke about his role, keeping his feelings from ever getting the least bit too serious.

"I'm the money guy," he said with a wink one time at a fund-raiser that Claire had organized. A big money guy, having raised more than $4 million for his foundation and the hospital. His foundation will put in another $500,000 for a second floor to the Weston-based center in 1999.

MARINO LIKES TO KEEP HIS PERSONAL LIFE — WELL, PERSONAL. WHEN HE
AND WIFE CLAIRE ADOPTED A 2-YEAR-OLD DAUGHTER FROM CHINA IN 1998
HE KEPT IT VERY LOW PROFILE.

Demand for the hospital is great. And why not? There are 70 medical professionals, from neurologists to speech and language pathologists, who handle 2,000 patients with neurological disorders every month.

All of that allowed Marino a rare moment of pride when he received the Man of the Year award.

"This award means a lot to me," he said. "I've achieved a lot of things in 16 years. But to be recognized for my work off the field for affecting people in a positive way means a lot. I'm very proud of what we've done with our foundation."

With his own children, he is similarly generous. Every year he packs up the family for a trip to Aspen, Colo. The children ski while Dad, whose injury-ravaged knees don't allow for the slopes, plays taxi driver.

"Yeah, I just drop them off in the morning, go work out and get lunch and then wait around to pick them up," he said with a laugh. "Try to keep it low-key as far as I'm concerned."

Low-key, perhaps. Private, perhaps. But great, without question.

BROTHERS IN ARMS

BY JIM KELLY

AS TOLD TO TIM O'SHEI

S o many superstar quarterbacks have come from my home area of Western Pennsylvania. There's Joe Montana, Johnny Unitas, Joe Namath, George Blanda...and there's Dan Marino.

Everybody wonders exactly what it is about the Pittsburgh region that produces all these top quarterbacks. I like to say it's the Iron City beer and the peanut butter and jelly sandwiches we ate. But there's something much more important: family. I know that for myself, for Joe Namath and for Dan, it was family values.

We learned that you have to work for anything you want badly, and we grew up with a hard-core willingness to make sacrifices. Whether it was the trophies for Punt, Pass & Kick or a new pair of shoes for basketball season, we had to earn it. In the winter, I'd shovel two feet of snow from the sidewalks of 15 neighbors. Come summer, I'd mow seven or eight lawns.

The way Dan and I were brought up is pretty similar: blue collar, having to fight and scratch and bite and do whatever it took to make ends meet. My dad was a machinist; Dan's dad drove a newspaper delivery truck. I grew up in a family of six boys; Dan had two younger

BY 1994, THE BILLS-DOLPHINS (AND KELLY-MARINO) RIVALRY WAS IN FULL FORCE. ALTHOUGH MARINO THREW FOR A COMBINED 523 YARDS IN TWO GAMES AGAINST HIS DIVISION RIVALS, BUFFALO WON TWICE.

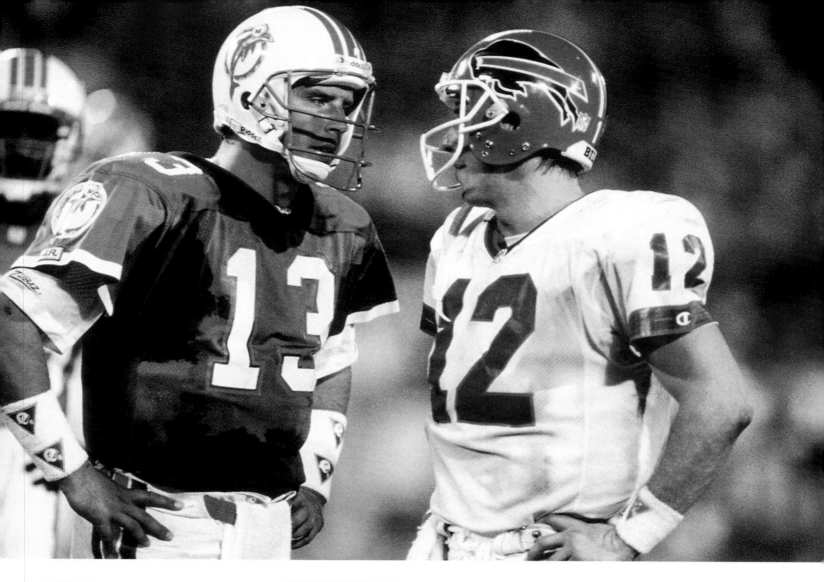

WHETHER IT WAS THE PUNT, PASS & KICK COMPETITION, OR A NEW PAIR OF SHOES, THE YOUNGSTERS OF WESTERN PENNSYLVANIA EARNED EVERYTHING THEY GOT. KELLY THINKS THAT MIND-SET CONTRIBUTED TO MARINO'S SUCCESS.

sisters. Dan grew up in the Oakland section of Pittsburgh and played his high school football in the city.

I played in East Brady, which is 60 miles from Pittsburgh, so we never played against each other. When I was a freshman, I heard about the quarterback from Central Catholic High. I never actually met Dan until the end of college in 1983, but I've seen him a lot since then.

People look back at the Class of '83 because there were six quarterbacks in the first round of the draft. In particular, there was the three of us: me, Dan and John Elway. What we were able to accomplish on the field has been written about in all the magazines. But what we were able to do as individuals for each other's charities is something significant, too. John, Dan and I have become good friends, attending each other's golf tournaments and helping one another in every way we can.

Throughout our NFL careers, Dan and I became good friends by attending so many charity events and appearances. Years ago, we had a couple of beers together at a Jack Lambert football camp, and it went from there. We didn't always talk football at these things, except when my teammate Bruce Smith was around. Dan would joke with Bruce about trying to sack him, and we'd come back at him by calling Joe Robbie Stadium by a different name: "Rich Stadium South." (Since we used to go down to Miami to kick their butts all the time, we renamed their field for the Buffalo Bills' stadium.)

Dan and I realize that friends come first, but when you get on the field, it's a different ballgame. And that's the way it should be. When you're in battle, everybody is your enemy … especially if that battle is between the Bills and the Dolphins. That whole rivalry began back in the 1970s, when Miami beat Buffalo in 20 straight games. (In fact, the Bills never beat the Dolphins in that decade.)

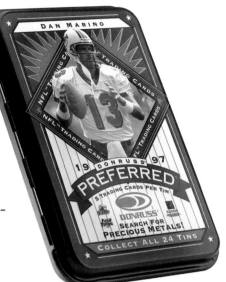

PACKS OF 1997 DONRUSS PREFERRED FOOTBALL CARDS WERE SOLD IN SMALL TINS WHICH HELD FIVE TRADING CARDS. THE TINS EACH FEATURED A DIFFERENT STAR PLAYER AND HAVE BECOME COLLECTIBLES THEMSELVES.

WHILE KELLY WAS PLAYING IN THE USFL IN 1983, MARINO WAS LIGHTING THE NFL WORLD ON FIRE, FINISHING THIRD IN QUARTERBACK RATING WHILE THROWING 20 TOUCHDOWN PASSES. INTERESTINGLY ENOUGH, BECAUSE OF INJURIES AND A LATE START MARINO PLAYED THE EQUIVALENT OF JUST 10 GAMES HIS ROOKIE SEASON.

MARINO QUICKLY DEVELOPED A REPUTATION FOR HAVING ONE OF THE QUICKEST RELEASES IN THE GAME. HIS GRACE UNDER RELENTLESS PRESSURE FROM OPPOSING LINEMEN IS ADMIRABLE, ESPECIALLY ON NOV. 12, 1995, WHEN HE CAUGHT A BATTED BALL, THUS COMPLETING A PASS TO HIMSELF, AGAINST NEW ENGLAND.

MARINO'S LIKENESS HAS BEEN USED ABOUT AS OFTEN AS ELVIS, "THE KING." THE 1996 STARTING LINEUP FOOTBALL FIGURE IS A CLASSIC MARINO POSE AND IS ONE OF 14 STARTING LINEUPS THAT HAVE BEEN MOLDED OF HIM TO DATE.

When I first came to Buffalo in 1986, one of the first goals we had was to improve to the point where we could beat the New York Jets and the Miami Dolphins. Since they were in our division, we knew we had to beat them to make the playoffs. It's always been a shootout, and it would often come down to the Bills and the Dolphins for a conference championship. There was a rivalry between Don Shula and Marv Levy; Jim Kelly and Dan Marino. (And a gentleman who helped take it to another level was Dan's former teammate, Bryan Cox. He helped us get even more pumped, because there was always something he said to elevate us that much more.)

I had some big games against the Dolphins. Dan had some big games against us. One of my favorite big-play games came in 1989 at Joe Robbie, when I dove across the goal line for a touchdown to win the game on the last play.

We had our share of tough games, but for every one, I never went out on the field and said, "OK, I'm playing against Dan Marino." I never went into a game thinking that. I went out there and said, "I'm playing against the Dolphins' defense. I can't do anything about stopping Dan Marino." But because of Dan, I knew that we were going to have to score points if we were going to beat them.

Now that John Elway has won a couple of Super Bowls, people ask me if I'd like to see Dan win one too. To a certain point, I would love to see Dan win a Super Bowl. Obviously, if it came down to another AFC Championship Game between the Bills and the Dolphins, I'd have to pull for Buffalo. But if Dan ever made it back to the Super Bowl, I'd be behind him 100 percent.

MARINO GREW UP IN THE OAKLAND SECTION OF PITTSBURGH, WHERE HIS FATHER DROVE A NEWSPAPER DELIVERY TRUCK. COMMON JOBS FOR YOUTHS INCLUDED SHOVELING SNOW IN THE WINTER AND MOWING LAWNS IN THE SUMMER, A LIFESTYLE THAT PREPARED DAN WELL FOR THE ROUGH LIFE OF AN NFL QUARTERBACK.

MARINO FIRST PLAYED AGAINST KELLY AND THE BUFFALO BILLS IN 1986.
IN TWO GAMES, MARINO THREW FOR 741 YARDS, AND THE DOLPHINS
WON TWICE.

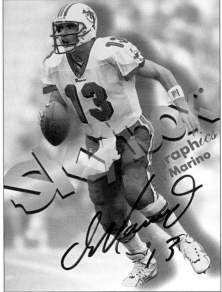

THE 1998 SKYBOX AUTOGRAPHICS SET INCLUDED THE AUTOGRAPHS OF 73 DIFFERENT PLAYERS, INCLUDING DAN MARINO. HIS AUTOGRAPH CARD IS THE MOST VALUABLE IN THE SET, ALONG WITH PHENOM RANDY MOSS.

JIM KELLY KNOWS WHAT IT FEELS LIKE TO FALL JUST SHORT OF A SUPER BOWL CHAMPIONSHIP. HIS BILLS LOST THE BIG GAME FOUR TIMES. NOW, HE SAYS HE'LL ROOT FOR MARINO IF THE DOLPHINS MAKE IT BACK TO THE SUPER BOWL.

STAYING POWER

BY ROGER STAUBACH
AS TOLD TO MICKEY SPAGNOLA

For Dan Marino to play this long, it takes a combination of physical and mental attributes. There are players who might be good quarterbacks who have had his injuries, but wouldn't have been able to fight through those injuries. You've got to deal with that.

I was fortunate. I had concussions, not knee problems, like John Elway. I think Elway would have played another year, but evidently, his knee is so bad he's limping around playing golf. Really, Marino has been somewhat the same. He's had the Achilles, the knee ... he's just a tough guy.

At that position, to deal with the physical part of the game, you have to be mentally disciplined. There are a lot of quarterbacks who are physically capable, but Dan is one of those rare breeds who is very mentally tough. He is a very disciplined type person in how he approaches his football, and he is very competitive and takes pride in what he does. And he also is blessed with that ability to execute. He has an outstanding arm, and has a delivery that is as good as anyone's.

Now that doesn't mean you are successful because of your delivery. Dan's ability to get rid of the ball quickly has put him at the fore-

> "I JUST LOVE TO BE OUT THERE PLAYING," MARINO SAYS. "WHEN YOU'RE AWAY FROM THE GAME, YOU DON'T TAKE IT FOR GRANTED."

A FIVE-TIME PRO BOWL QUARTER-BACK, ROGER STAUBACH LED THE COWBOYS TO SIX NFC CHAMPIONSHIP GAMES AND FOUR SUPER BOWLS WHILE IN DALLAS (1969–1979). ELECTED TO THE PRO FOOTBALL HALL OF FAME IN 1985, STAUBACH WAS A STELLAR PER-FORMER IN THE CLUTCH, LEADING THE COWBOYS TO 23 COMEBACK VICTORIES.

front of that category, which keeps down the sacks. And he also is very accurate. So physically, he's blessed.

But still, he's played through injuries. That's where the mental toughness comes in. And you have to be able to play through injuries to be a quarterback this long. He just has the whole package. And he's not just a quarterback with longevity, he's a superstar quarterback who's had longevity, and that's not easy to do. That's because playing quarterback puts you into a situation where you get more credit than you deserve and you also get more criticism. But to continue to play at his level for so long, you've got to be mentally disci-plined, especially with the kinds of injuries he's had. To me, fighting through injuries is mental toughness.

Really, you see some quarterbacks today who aren't in the mode of a Troy Aikman or Elway or Marino. Physically, sure, they are very, very good. But they just can't deal with all the issues that relate to being a quarterback. The pressures of being a quarterback and the mental side of the game. And that mental side includes not making mistakes on the field, and, again, not just the mental toughness it takes to lead your team over the goal line, but the ability to understand what's going on out there. I mean, it's probably the difference of six or seven plays between a Marino and an also-ran, an Aikman and an also-ran in the league. And Marino is definitely someone who knows what's going on out there and makes very few mistakes. There are a lot of players who have physical talent but can't transfer that talent into being the type of quarterback Dan Marino is.

Then to play this long, you have to have those juices inside you, too. I was 38 when I retired, and would have loved to play 20 years, but it wouldn't have worked. You really enjoy that competition. Football is, hopefully with the playoffs, a 19-game season, so you really miss that routine.

MARINO HAS UNDERGONE SURGERY ON HIS LEFT KNEE FIVE TIMES SINCE JOINING THE DOLPHINS. THE MOST RECENT OF THOSE WAS SURGERY TO REPAIR LOOSE CARTILAGE IN 1991. THE OTHER KNEE OPERATIONS WERE PERFORMED IN 1988, 1986, 1985 AND 1984.

ON OCT. 10, 1993, MARINO WENT DOWN WITH A TORN RIGHT ACHILLES TENDON AS HE SCRAMBLED TO AVOID THE BROWN'S RUSH IN THE MIAMI-CLEVELAND GAME. HE HAD ENTERED THE GAME AS THE NFL'S MOST DURABLE QUARTERBACK, PLAYING IN 145 CONSECUTIVE GAMES DATING BACK TO 1984.

As long as they are physically able, most quarterbacks want to play as long as they can. Now today, if you're on a team, you can't do it by yourself. I mean, Archie Manning was a magnificent quarterback who never was really surrounded by good players. If you're in the right situation, and there's that desire to go out each week to fight and win the game, you can play a long time.

I miss the heck out of that, and what I miss the most is that feeling you have inside when you've beaten somebody. So I think that's what drives a Marino or an Elway to keep playing.

And with Marino, there are times when I don't know how he does it. His mobility has left him. But he has such a great arm, and if you have the kind of protection you should have and you have a running game, which Miami is trying to develop, you can still be a magnificent quarterback with his arm. And that's why quarterbacks can hang around longer.

Also, the game has changed, and the experience you have when you are looking at all the different defensive sets, and understanding what's going on over there, is so important. The game still comes down to six or seven plays. So if you have the experience, and are physically able, that's a good formula today. For the young guys coming in, it's so complicated for them, so the experienced quarterback, as long as he's capable, is very valuable to a football team today.

I just think Marino has been magnificent at doing all of this. Now some people might want to talk about Dan not winning Super Bowls, but all the stars have to come together to win one. I don't think that should be the final judgment. Sure it's part, but not the main thing. I think if Marino doesn't win a Super Bowl, people will look at that. "He couldn't win a Super Bowl." But I think it's unjust. I don't think it's right.

I still would have said John Elway was a great quarterback, even though he had taken Denver teams to the Super Bowls and didn't win them. To me, you could have matched him up on an even basis with anybody. But now that he's won the two, everybody is making him out to be that great quarterback he always was.

Marino will transcend that. I don't think that will be his legacy. And I wouldn't want that to be Jim Kelly's legacy, either. I think Jim Kelly was a great quarterback. There is a guy who played hurt. Kelly was a heck of a quarterback. No, that should not be a quarterback's legacy. And I don't think it will be Marino's — just so many years of playing at a high level.

Now if he does win one, that's going to be nice. That won't be easy — he might be the Ronald Reagan of quarterbacks if he does. I guess he has a few more years left in him, but to tell you the truth, I don't know how he does it.

TO SEE DAN UP-CLOSE YOU HAVE TO LOOK NO FURTHER THAN THE 1998 RIDDELL GAME GREATS. AN ACTUAL PHOTOGRAPH OF MARINO'S FACE IS STRETCHED 360° TO CREATE THE COLLECTIBLE.

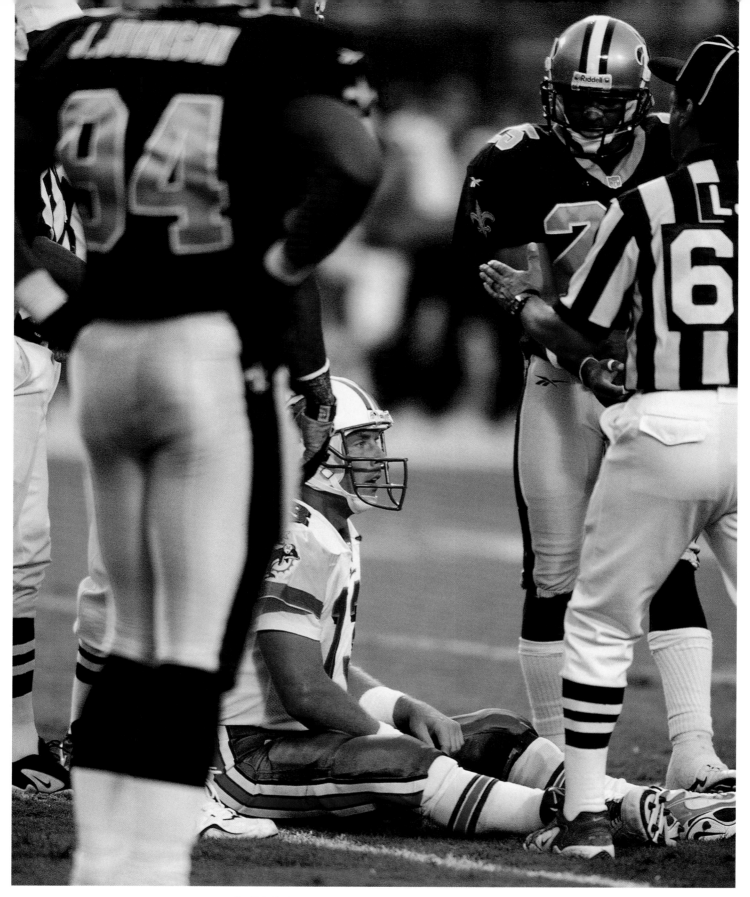

IN 1992 MARINO WASN'T GIVEN MUCH PROTECTION IN THE POCKET; HE
WAS SACKED A CAREER-HIGH 28 TIMES. ON NOV. 29 IN A GAME AGAINST
THE SAINTS HE WAS SACKED FIVE TIMES, THE MOST TIMES HE HAD BEEN
SACKED IN A SINGLE GAME IN HIS CAREER.

ONE OF THE TOP SACK ARTISTS IN PRO FOOTBALL, NEIL SMITH, DROPPED
MARINO IN THE CHIEFS' 1990 AFC WILD CARD PLAYOFF LOSS AT MIAMI.
THAT SACK MARKED THE ONLY TIME SMITH HAS MANAGED TO TAKE
DOWN MARINO AND HIS QUICK RELEASE.

Maybe the best thing you can say about Dan is, when you are watching a game, you still feel there is some way this guy is going to pull it out. I mean, he's still going to be fun to watch even if the score is 21–0 at halftime. You say, "Well Marino is there; he can figure it out." While in other games you say, "Well that game is over," and if you have DIRECTV you turn to the next one. But if a Marino, or an Elway, or an Aikman, or a Steve Young is playing, you just feel they can make something still happen. He's that good … still that good.

BEFORE HIS ACHILLES INJURY IN '93, MARINO WAS THE ONLY NFL QUARTERBACK TO HAVE STARTED EVERY GAME SINCE THE REPLACEMENT GAMES IN 1987. THAT STREAK ALSO PUT HIM ON THE LIST OF ONLY FIVE NFL QBS WHO HAVE STARTED 100 OR MORE CONSECUTIVE GAMES.

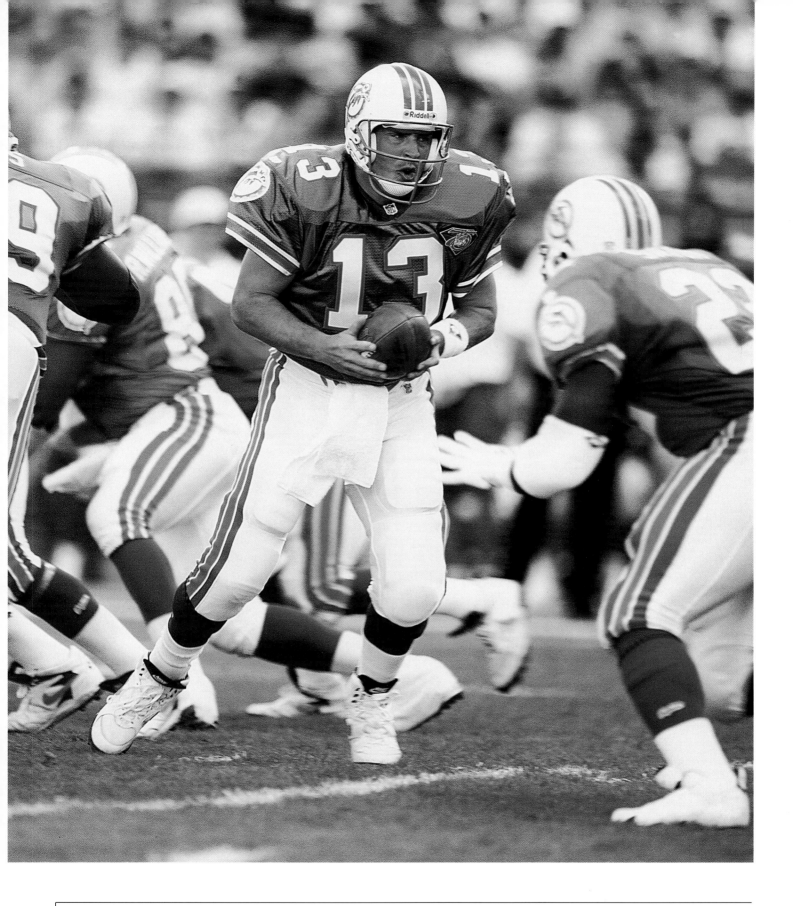

"IF I'M A COACH, I'M THINKING, 'IF WE DON'T DO SOMETHING TO SLOW THIS GUY DOWN, I'M GOING TO END UP FIRED,' " SAYS BRUCE SMITH, DEFENSIVE END FOR THE BUFFALO BILLS. "YOU JUST CAN'T SAY ENOUGH ABOUT THE GUY. HE JUST PUTS UP NUMBERS THAT ARE PHENOMENAL. HE REALLY IS YOUR WORST NIGHTMARE."

MARINO HAS BEEN A TESTAMENT TO LONGEVITY AND TOUGHNESS FOR THE DOLPHINS. HE HAS PLAYED MORE SEASONS AND GAMES FOR THE TEAM THAN ANY OTHER PLAYER HAS IN DOLPHINS' HISTORY.

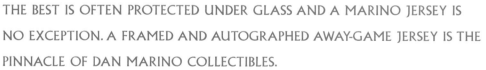

THE BEST IS OFTEN PROTECTED UNDER GLASS AND A MARINO JERSEY IS NO EXCEPTION. A FRAMED AND AUTOGRAPHED AWAY-GAME JERSEY IS THE PINNACLE OF DAN MARINO COLLECTIBLES.

TO HANG UP YOUR FAVORITE PHOTOS OF MARINO ON YOUR REFRIGERATOR, TRY A DIE-CUT DAN MARINO MAGNET MADE BY CROWNPRO ENTERPRISES.

THE LEGACY

BY JIMMY JOHNSON
AS TOLD TO JASON COLE

I'm not really good at comparing people, but I think Dan, without question, is one of the greatest quarterbacks to play this game. I'm not a historian, so I can't compare him to some of the great quarterbacks of yesteryear, or guys I haven't personally seen. But Dan has had a great career.

You're talking about a player who really changed the game. Dan's play early in his career made coaches change their way of thinking about the passing game, both offensively and defensively.

When I got here, it was a slightly different situation. It'd been changing even before that. I think between some injuries he had and the way other teams had started to play, Dan realized before I got here — and he realized it even more after I got here — that in order for us to be successful, we have to be somewhat balanced by running the ball.

And by running the ball, that will make his job that much easier. His numbers have gone down since I got here, but that was a factor of change. We still could have been throwing as much as the Dolphins did before I got here. His numbers would have stayed about the same. But how long would we have had him here? Sacrificing some numbers to get to where we need to be as a team is a good idea in this situation, and Dan was on board with that. I know he was frustrated sometimes,

AFTER AN EARLY ADJUSTMENT PERIOD, MARINO HAS FLOURISHED IN JIMMY JOHNSON'S OFFENSE. HE THREW FOR 3,780 YARDS IN 1997, RIGHT IN LINE WITH THE NUMBERS HE POSTED IN THE LATE 1980s.

and I should have made an even bigger change to start with to get us further along.

I thought that my idea of emphasizing the run and playing good defense would be enough. It wasn't. We were still relying too much on Dan when the going got rough, and it hurt us. Our playoff game in New England (in 1997) was a primary example. We relied almost entirely on Dan and our receivers, and our running game wasn't enough to help him. The Patriots figured out what we were doing. They did it so well, they even knew our audibles.

Now, when Dan was at his very best and had the style of offense that was suited for throwing the football, they were able to put up a lot of big numbers. But, even then, there were those setbacks when either he was off or there was bad weather or the receivers were dropping balls. So he knew before I got here that we had to run the ball.

But the fact that Dan was able to do that style of offense for so long is a tribute to him. Very few players can handle that burden. Dan was a great player, and the offense was built around him. Players were drafted and signed based on whether their style suited his talents — the style of offensive linemen for pass protection, the pass receivers …

The emphasis was on the passing game, and even the amount of time in practice spent on the passing game was extraordinary. So Dan was such a great talent that the Dolphins used that talent by building the team around him.

Unfortunately, that didn't work for them, and I think people have started to make too much out of that in terms of Dan's legacy. People

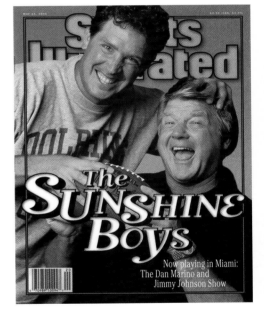

WHEN DAN AND JIMMY SHARED THE MAY 13, 1996, *SPORTS ILLUSTRATED* COVER IT WAS ALL SMILES. IT MARKED THE EIGHTH *SI* COVER APPEARANCE FOR MARINO AND SECOND FOR JIMMY JOHNSON.

[119]

talk about the Super Bowl and Dan needing to have won one. I don't think having a ring is indicative of individual talent. Individually, there are some great, great players who don't have rings. Individuals don't win rings, teams do. Joe Montana won a bunch of rings, and Joe Montana was a great quarterback. But Joe Montana was part of some great San Francisco teams. So Dan not winning a ring up to this point, that isn't a knock on him at all.

MARINO IMMEDIATELY IMPRESSED NEW COACH JIMMY JOHNSON WITH HIS WILLINGNESS TO SACRIFICE PERSONAL ACCOMPLISHMENTS FOR THE GOOD OF THE TEAM. JOHNSON READILY ADMITS HIS QB IS ONE OF THE BEST EVER.

THE TOUCHDOWN SIGNAL IS NOTHING NEW TO MARINO. TO PICK UP THIS PIECE, FANS HAD TO PURCHASE IT AT THE EAST COAST STARTING LINEUP CONVENTION NOV. 7–8, 1998, IN EDISON, N.J.

JIMMY JOHNSON'S CHANGE IN
PHILOSOPHY RESULTED IN SOME
VERY UN-MARINO-LIKE NUMBERS
IN 1996. DAN THREW JUST 17
TOUCHDOWN PASSES, HIS FEWEST IN
ANY PREVIOUS YEAR IN WHICH HE
PLAYED MORE THAN FIVE GAMES.

The teams he played on were just flawed. They didn't have the running game to win it, and they didn't emphasize it enough. When you get late into a season, you need to be able to control games with the running game. You get into so much bad weather, particularly on the road in this division (the AFC East), that you have to be able to grind.

The thing that has been interesting for me to watch is how much Dan has accepted the change in the team. Obviously, a lot of this wasn't going to be comfortable for him. A lot of the people he was used to seeing, the veteran players, are gone, and it's a whole new group of guys. Younger guys.

We've turned this team over pretty good. When I was in Dallas, a lot of the older players didn't like it when I brought in a bunch of young players. They were used to having a veteran team. Eventually, when they didn't help make it work, they were gone, too.

MARINO EXPERIENCED A REBIRTH OF SORTS UNDER JOHNSON IN 1997. DAN THREW FOR 3,780 YARDS, NEARLY 1,000 MORE THAN THE SEASON BEFORE.

Dan has been behind this the whole way. We did some things early to keep certain people on offense, veteran players, but even that has changed. He has understood and helped make it work. I don't know how much he has socialized with the younger guys. They're just different people. But he has been good with them in the locker room. In the past, Dan could be a pretty intimidating presence and it took a guy with a veteran attitude to handle that. But he has really been accepting.

Some of the on-field intensity, he's put that away a little bit to keep the young guys from going into a shell if they make a mistake. In that way, he has become a really important leader for what we're doing and what he's trying to accomplish at the end of his career.

EARLY IN HIS CAREER, 49ERS QUARTERBACK STEVE YOUNG HAD SOMETHING MARINO NEVER REALLY HAS HAD: AN EFFECTIVE RUNNING GAME. AT LEAST PARTLY BECAUSE OF THAT, YOUNG LEADS MARINO IN SUPER BOWLS WON, 1-0.

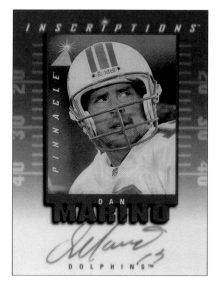

DAN SIGNED A TOTAL OF 440 1997 PINNACLE INSCRIPTIONS AUTOGRAPH CARDS AS PART OF A 30-CARD AUTOGRAPH SET RELEASED BY PINNACLE BRANDS. ALL OF THE SIGNERS IN THE SET WERE QUARTERBACK CLUB MEMBERS AND THE CARDS WERE MADE OF A CLEAR PLASTIC.

MARINO VS. HALL OF FAME QUARTERBACKS

(Comparing Dan Marino's career, through 1998, with those of the 18 quarterbacks in the Pro Football Hall of Fame.)

PLAYER	ATT	COMP	YDS	PCT	TD	INT	RATE
DAN MARINO	7,989	4,763	58,913	59.6	408	235	87.3
SAMMY BAUGH	2,995	1,693	21,886	56.5	186	203	72.0
GEORGE BLANDA	4,007	1,911	25,920	47.7	236	277	60.7
TERRY BRADSHAW	3,901	2,025	27,989	51.9	212	210	71.1
LEN DAWSON	3,741	2,136	28,711	57.6	239	183	82.6
DAN FOUTS	5,604	3,297	43,040	59.0	254	242	80.2
OTTO GRAHAM	1,565	872	13,499	55.7	88	94	78.2
BOB GRIESE	3,429	1,926	25,092	56.2	192	172	77.1
SONNY JURGENSEN	4,262	2,433	32,224	57.1	255	189	82.0
BOBBY LAYNE	3,700	1,814	26,768	49.0	196	243	63.4
SID LUCKMAN	1,744	904	14,683	51.8	139	131	75.7
JOE NAMATH	3,762	1,886	27,663	50.1	173	220	65.6
BART STARR	3,149	1,803	24,718	57.4	152	138	80.3
ROGER STAUBACH	2,958	1,685	22,700	57.0	153	109	83.4
FRAN TARKENTON	6,467	3,686	47,003	57.0	342	266	80.4
Y.A. TITTLE	4,395	2,427	33,070	55.2	242	248	74.4
JOHNNY UNITAS	5,186	2,830	40,239	54.6	290	253	78.2
NORM VAN BROCKLIN	2,895	1,553	23,611	53.6	173	178	75.1
BOB WATERFIELD	1,617	814	11,849	50.3	98	127	61.6

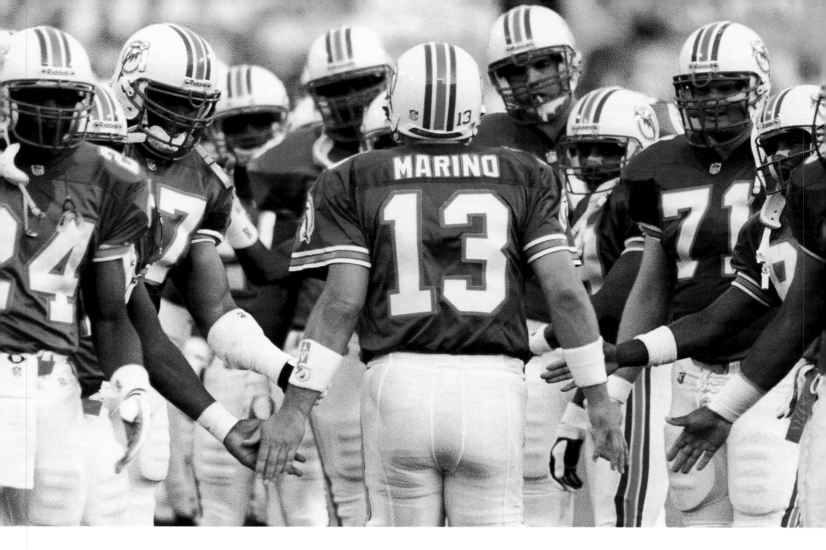

Book design by David Timmons.

EDITORIAL CREDITS

Mickey Spagnola, who interviewed Troy Aikman and Roger Staubach, covers the Dallas Cowboys for *The Insider*.

Kevin Kaminski, who interviewed Don Shula, covers the Miami Dolphins for *Dolphins Digest*.

Vic Carucci, who interviewed Phil Simms and contributed the Class of His Own chapter, covers the Bills for the *Buffalo News*.

Pat Livingston, who contributed the Youth Movement and College Try chapters, is a Pittsburgh-based freelance writer.

Jason Cole, who interviewed Jimmy Johnson and contributed the On the Sidelines chapter, covers the Miami Dolphins for the *Ft. Lauderdale Sun-Sentinel*.

Tim O'Shei, who interviewed Jim Kelly, is a freelance writer in the Buffalo area.

PHOTO CREDITS

AP/Wide World Photos: 33, 126; Vernon Biever: 104; Mike Dehoog/TDP: 71, 121; Tom DiPace: 1, 2, 4, 5, 6, 11, 34, 39, 40, 41, 42, 44, 46, 50, 52, 54, 62, 64, 65, 66, 68, 72, 73, 76, 79, 88, 92, 93, 94, 95, 97, 98, 99, 101, 102, 106, 108, 109, 110, 111, 112, 113, 115, 116, 120, 122, 123, 124, 125; Kobal Collection: 78; Anthony Neste: 22; NFL Photos: 14, 17, 32, 38, 90; Pittsburgh Post-Gazette: 18 bottom, 20 top right, 21, 25 bottom, 26, 30, 31; Bob Rosato: 8, 12, 37, 100; Marc Serota: 48, 67, 80, 81, 82, 83, 85, 86, 105, 118, 128; Sports Illustrated: 10, 36, 49, 55, 56, 57; University of Pittsburgh: 24, 25 top, 27, 28, 29; Yearbook Archives: 15, 16, 18 top, 19 top, 20 left, 20 bottom

Tim Franz and Rudy Klancnik provided Dan Marino memorabilia for this book.